BEYOND THE BOTTOM LINE

BEYOND THE BOTTOM LINE

A Step-by-Step Guide to Building a Profitable and Purpose-Driven Business

JENNIFER K. RIDER

Dedication

To my family, friends, and colleagues – your encouragement and belief in me gave me the confidence to put pen to paper and share my approach to doing business. Thank you for pushing me to capture these ideas, to refine them, and to create a framework that can help others navigate the path to a more purposeful way of leading.

To Blake de Vos – for giving me the structure, guidance, and accountability I needed to transform these ideas into a book. Your insights and expertise helped bring clarity to my vision, and for that, I am deeply grateful.

And most importantly, to you, the reader – the leader, the changemaker, the one willing to take a stand and do things differently. You know that purpose and profit aren't at odds; they are the foundation of long-term success. You believe in leading with intention, making a difference, and proving that business can be a force for good.

This book is for you – because the future of business belongs to those who dare to reimagine what's possible.

Here's to building a world where everyone, everywhere can thrive.

THE NET-POSITIVITY FRAMEWORK

TOOLKIT

Want to turn purpose into action?

Get the Net-Positivity Toolkit – free templates, exercises, and tools to turn your mission into action.

www.hera-associates.com/toolkit-download

Copyright © 2025 Jennifer K. Rider

All rights reserved. No part of this publication may be reproduced, stored in a retrieval system, or transmitted in any form or by any means – electronic, mechanical, photocopying, recording, or otherwise – without the prior written permission of the publisher, except in the case of brief quotations embodied in critical articles or reviews.

Published by Impact Group Publishing
www.impactgrouppublishing.com

ISBN: 978-1-7641084-0-9

Cover design by Tess McCabe.
Editing by Michele Perry.
Typesetting by Kerry Milin.

This book is a work of nonfiction. Every effort has been made to ensure accuracy, but the author and publisher accept no liability for errors or omissions.

Disclaimer: The content of this book is based on the author's professional experience and is provided for general educational and informational purposes. While every effort has been made to ensure accuracy, this publication is not intended to replace personalised business, financial, or legal advice specific to your situation.

Readers are encouraged to seek independent advice where appropriate.
The author and publisher disclaim any liability arising directly or indirectly from the use of this material. Business outcomes are influenced by many variables, and results may vary.

For more information, visit: www.hera-associates.com

Contents

Introduction: A New Era of Business — 1

PART I: THE WHY — 7
Understanding Net-Positivity

1. Why Net-Positivity Matters Now — 9
2. The Business Case for Balancing Profit and Purpose — 19
3. Unpacking the Net-Positivity Framework — 25

PART II: THE HOW — 37
Building the Foundation

4. Pillar 1: Strategic Purpose-Driven Vision
   Defining Your Purpose — 39
5. Pillar 2: Sustainable Purpose-Driven Operations
   Aligning Your Processes with Your Mission — 59
6. Pillar 3: Data-Driven Measurement
   Measuring What Matters — 79
7. Pillar 4: Collaborative Leadership
   Building Teams and Cultures that Drive Impact — 103

PART III: THE WHAT
Taking Action   113

8 Tools for Transformation   115
   Sustainability Audits, KPI Trackers, and DEI Roadmaps

9 Real-World Success Stories   129
   Lessons From Net-Positive Leaders

10 Sector Spotlights   143
   Tailoring Strategies for Your Business Type

11 Staying the Course   173
   Long-Term Planning and Adaptability

12 Leading the Way   191
   Becoming a Champion for Net-Positivity

13 Creating a Legacy   205
   Leaving a Lasting Impact on Your Business and the World

Conclusion: Leading the Future   223

Let's Keep the Momentum Going   227

Acknowledgments   229

About the Author   231

Introduction
A New Era of Business

Did you know that businesses with a strong sense of purpose outperform their competitors by 42 percent[1] – and yet most leaders still struggle to balance profit with impact?

A truth I've learned over nearly three decades of working in responsive programming, social-impact delivery, and business transformation: the businesses that thrive in the long run don't just chase profit – they align it with "purpose." I've seen this firsthand in roles where I've guided companies through transformational growth, strengthened financial sustainability, and designed strategies that empower businesses to make meaningful societal influence. Whether restructuring revenue models for resilience or partnering with leaders to scale purpose-driven operations, my career has been rooted in one core belief: when businesses commit to making a positive impact, everyone wins.

Over 25 years, I've partnered with businesses – startups, corporations, and nonprofits – to navigate the complexities of growth, resilience, and profitability in a rapidly changing world. From helping Big Brothers Big Sisters increase market share by 55 percent to leading multimillion-dollar fundraising campaigns at the YMCA, my work has always centered on solving big problems with actionable solutions. One of my

---

1 Development Dimensions International, The Conference Board, and EY. *Global Leadership Forecast 2018: 25 Research Insights to Fuel Your People Strategy*. 2018, media.ddiworld.com/research/global-leadership-forecast-2018_ddi_tr.pdf.

most transformative projects has been co-founding Hera Associates, a social-impact consulting firm that began as a side hustle and has grown into a thriving government-contracting business.

At Hera Associates, we specialize in helping organizations – public and private – embed purpose into their strategies to drive sustainable growth and measurable effects. In just a few years, we've worked with nonprofits, midsized businesses, and government agencies to integrate diversity, equity, inclusion, and social impact into their operations. From securing state contracts to advising on federal climate adaptation projects, Hera Associates has grown into a trusted partner for leaders committed to balancing profit with purpose. Transitioning this venture from a side project into a full-time endeavor taught me firsthand what it takes to scale a mission-driven business while navigating the challenges of government contracting, stakeholder engagement, and operational complexity.

These experiences have given me a deep understanding of how businesses can thrive by aligning their values with their strategies – whether through diversifying revenue streams, implementing data-driven decision-making, or fostering inclusive cultures that empower teams. The lessons I've learned through Hera Associates, combined with decades of leadership across diverse sectors, have shaped the practical tools and insights I share in this book.

Now, I want to pass those insights onto you.

I wrote this book because I have seen a growing desire among business leaders – especially new-generation entrepreneurs and executives – to redefine what success looks like. Profit-at-all-costs is an outdated model. Today's leaders want to build businesses that are not only financially successful but also socially engaging and environmentally sustainable.

Let's explore two different scenarios from two different types of businesses – one: a midsized apparel company looking to connect with customers and employees; the other: a large human-services organization navigating the dual crises of a pandemic and financial uncertainty – to see how aligning purpose with operations can transform not just outcomes but entire cultures.

A few years ago, I worked with a midsized apparel company that was struggling to attract new customers and retain its best employees. They came to me, frustrated, saying, "We make a good product; we pay competitive salaries, so why are we losing people and customers to competitors?"

After digging in, we realized the business lacked a sense of purpose beyond the bottom line. Customers wanted to know the company cared about sustainability. Employees wanted to feel like their work contributed to something meaningful. By helping them shift their strategy – reducing waste in their operations, creating a community partnership program, and measuring their impact – the company not only improved its bottom line but also became an employer and brand of choice. Within a year, they saw a 20 percent increase in customer loyalty and a significant boost in employee retention.

The other example comes from my role as part of the executive leadership team running a tri-county, $160-million human-service organization during a pivotal moment. At the height of the pandemic, the organization faced a 60 percent revenue loss, staff burnout, and a community in desperate need of support. It would have been easy to focus solely on financial survival, but we took a different approach: we leaned into the organization's purpose. We restructured operations to ensure financial sustainability while prioritizing programs that addressed economic mobility and family stability – issues that had never been more urgent. By forming innovative partnerships with local governments and corporations, we impacted over 20,000 individuals annually, proving that when businesses (or organizations) lead with purpose, they not only endure – they thrive.

This experience, like so many others, showed me what's possible when leaders *align profit with purpose.*

But let's be honest: knowing where to start or how to integrate these goals into a business strategy can feel overwhelming.

That's where this book comes in.

This book is for business leaders who are ready to move beyond "business as usual."

Whether you're an entrepreneur seeking to differentiate your brand, a corporate executive balancing shareholder demands with sustainability goals, or a small business owner striving to align profitability with purpose, you'll find practical answers here. You'll learn how to align profit with purpose, embed social impact into your business strategy, and measure success in ways that resonate with customers, employees, and investors.

So, Why Now?

Because the stakes have never been higher.

Consumers, employees, and investors are demanding transparency, equity, and accountability. Businesses that can't meet these expectations risk becoming irrelevant. Meanwhile, leaders who adapt to this shift will find themselves at the forefront of a revolution in business – one that balances profitability with creating a better world.

In this book, I'll introduce the **Net-Positivity Framework**, a step-by-step guide to transforming your business into a purpose-driven powerhouse.

Let's look at Patagonia, for example – a company that built its success by embedding purpose into every facet of its operations. By prioritizing sustainability, ethical supply chains, and environmental activism, they not only earned the trust and loyalty of customers but also achieved consistent financial growth. Their story proves a powerful truth: businesses that align profit with purpose don't just survive – they *thrive*.

Through actionable tools, real-world case studies, and clear strategies, this book will show you how to integrate social impact into your daily operations. You'll learn how to craft a vision that inspires, foster collaborative leadership, measure impact in meaningful ways, and build a resilient business that stands the test of time.

By the end of this journey, you'll not only understand what it means to lead a net-positive business – you'll feel confident and equipped to make it happen.

This book isn't just about improving your bottom line; it's about reshaping the future of business. Together, we'll redefine success, ensuring that your business thrives financially while making a meaningful difference in the world.

So ...

Let's get started – because the future of business depends on leaders like *you*.

What kind of legacy do you want your business to leave behind?

How can you thrive financially while making a meaningful impact on your employees, your community, and the world?

You hold the power to redefine what success looks like – not just for your business, but for future generations.

This book is your guide to that transformation.

Just as I've seen businesses overcome challenges by aligning profit with purpose, I know you can too. Whether you're looking to strengthen your company's resilience, engage a more purpose-driven workforce, or stand out in a competitive market, the **Net-Positivity Framework** will help you turn those aspirations into reality. Together, we'll navigate this journey so you can achieve the kind of success that truly matters: financial growth that leaves a lasting, positive impact.

The future is calling.

Are you ready to answer?

PART I
THE WHY

Understanding Net-Positivity

Before we dive into the "how" of building a net-positive business, we need to explore the "why." In this section, we'll break down why purpose is no longer optional for businesses that want to succeed. From shifting consumer expectations to increasing pressure for transparency, the business landscape is changing fast. The companies that lead with impact are thriving, while those clinging to outdated models risk being left behind. These chapters will help you understand the forces driving this transformation and set the foundation for integrating purpose into your business strategy.

1

Why Net-Positivity Matters Now

A few years ago, I found myself standing in the checkout line, debating a simple choice: two nearly identical products – one from a big-name brand, the other from a company committed to sustainability. The difference? A few extra dollars and the promise that my purchase would support fair wages and eco-friendly production. In that moment, I realized something substantial was happening – people, including me, were no longer just buying products; we were choosing *values*.

That's when it hit me: the way we do business has changed, and companies that fail to recognize this shift aren't just missing an opportunity – they're writing their own exit strategy.

Businesses that fail to adapt to the expectations of today's world risk losing not just their customers, but their relevance. The question isn't whether you can afford to prioritize purpose – it's whether you can afford not to.

The Shift in Business as Usual

For decades, businesses operated under a single, unrelenting focus: maximizing profit. Shareholders demanded it, systems incentivized it, and leaders delivered it. But the tides have shifted. Today's business landscape is not the same as it was ten, or even five years ago. The old model – "profit-at-all-costs" – is no longer sustainable. Consumers, employees, investors, and society at large are demanding something more.

Why has this shift happened, and more importantly, why does it matter?

The answer lies in three powerful, interconnected forces that are redefining how businesses operate and how they're measured.

First, the climate and social crisis has become impossible to ignore. We are living in a time of unprecedented challenges: climate change, widening income inequality, resource scarcity, and deep systemic inequities. These problems are no longer abstract; they are affecting communities, economies, and daily lives around the world. People are demanding action, and businesses are being called to step up. For leaders, this is a critical moment.

Ignore these issues – you risk reputational and financial damage.

Act boldly – you can position your business as part of the solution: a leader driving meaningful change in a world that desperately needs it.

At the same time, a new generation of consumers and employees is demanding more. Millennials and Gen Z – who now make up the majority of both the workforce and the consumer market – aren't just looking for products or paychecks. They're looking for alignment of values. They care about how businesses operate, how products are made, and whether companies are making a positive impact on society and the environment.

Nearly 90 percent of Gen Z believe businesses must take action on social and environmental issues, and they vote with their wallets and their loyalty. If your business doesn't align with their expectations, they'll move on to one that does – no matter how strong your product or service might be.

Finally, technology and transparency have completely changed the game. In today's hyperconnected world, where social media and instant communication dominate, no business can hide. Every decision you make is amplified, analyzed, and judged in real time. Poor practices, unsustainable operations, or tone-deaf messaging can go viral in an instant, and the damage can be swift and lasting. But this new level of visibility is also an opportunity. Businesses that prioritize purpose, act with integrity, and demonstrate measurable impact can build trust, attract loyalty, and stand out in an increasingly competitive landscape. Those that don't, risk losing relevance, credibility, and customers.

At first glance, it may seem as though the largest, most entrenched corporations – those with deep pockets and monopolizing influence – are still driving the market. But the reality is far more dynamic. It's the nimble, innovative companies that are rewriting the rules of business and influencing the future. These companies are quick to adapt, integrating purpose into their strategy while finding smarter, more sustainable ways to operate. They're listening to what consumers and employees want, and they're shaping industries by setting new standards of accountability, impact, and success.

Why does this matter?

Because the rules of business have changed. Climate pressures, rising expectations, and a demand for transparency have created a new playing field – one where purpose and profit must go hand in hand. Leaders who embrace this shift will thrive, building stronger businesses that are not only financially successful but also leave a lasting, positive impact on the world.

The question is: will you lead the change, or will you be left behind?

Consider this: 70 percent of consumers say they are more likely to support brands that reflect their values and demonstrate a commitment to social or environmental good.² The message is clear – people want to spend their money on companies that care about more than the bottom line. A business that ignores this shift is at risk of losing not just customers, but loyalty, trust, and future growth.

If your business disappeared tomorrow, would your community or the world feel the loss?

It's a sobering thought, but it's one that leaders today must confront. Businesses that embrace a purpose beyond profit create lasting value – not just for themselves but for their customers, employees, and stakeholders. That's what "net-positivity" is all about: a balance of financial success and measurable societal impact.

To understand why net-positivity matters right now, let's look more closely at three forces driving this transformation.

1. Consumer behavior has changed

Today's consumers are informed, empowered, and intentional about where they spend their money. They're not just buying products; they're buying into stories, values, and trust. A recent Nielsen report found that 73 percent of global consumers are willing to pay more for sustainable products. This isn't a niche trend – it's a fundamental shift.

Brands like Patagonia, for example, have succeeded not only because of their quality but because they align with their customers' values. Patagonia's bold decisions – like pledging one percent of its profits to environmental causes – aren't just acts of charity; they're acts of strategy. The result? Unparalleled brand loyalty, strong financial performance, and a fiercely loyal customer base.

---

2   Edelman. *2019 Edelman Trust Barometer Special Report: In Brands We Trust?* Edelman, 2019, www.edelman.com/sites/g/files/aatuss191/files/2019-07/2019_edelman_trust_barometer_special_report_in_brands_we_trust_executive_summary.pdf.
"Optimove Surveys: 70% of Consumers Prefer Eco-Friendly Brands as 64% of Brands Say They Have an Environmental Responsibility Program." PR Newswire, 20 June 2023, www.prnewswire.com/news-releases/optimove-surveys-70-of-consumers-prefer-eco-friendly-brands-as-64-of-brands-say-they-have-an-environmental-responsibility-program-301851861.html.

For businesses that fail to adapt to this demand, the risk is clear: irrelevance. Brands that can't demonstrate purpose are easily replaced by those that can. Consider the story of Forever 21, a retail giant that once dominated the fast-fashion market. For years, its business model focused on offering inexpensive, trend-driven clothing to consumers at a rapid pace. However, as consumer priorities shifted toward sustainability and ethical production, Forever 21 failed to adapt. While competitors like H&M and Zara launched conscious collections and publicly committed to sustainability goals, Forever 21 largely ignored growing concerns about environmental impact, labor practices, and corporate responsibility.

The result?

A dramatic decline in customer loyalty and sales.

In 2019, Forever 21 filed for bankruptcy, closing hundreds of stores worldwide. Meanwhile, brands that aligned with their customers' values – like Reformation – flourished, attracting consumers who were willing to pay more for sustainable, purpose-driven fashion.

This example illustrates a hard truth: businesses that fail to meet evolving consumer expectations risk becoming irrelevant. Today's consumers are not just buying products; they're investing in brands that reflect their values. Businesses that don't adapt will lose market share to those that do.

2. Employees expect more

The war for talent is real, and businesses that fail to meet the expectations of today's workforce are losing. Gone are the days when employees were motivated solely by paychecks. Purpose, impact, and belonging are now top priorities. In fact, a Deloitte study found that 44 percent of Millennials and Gen Z employees have turned down jobs because they didn't align with their values.[3]

---

3   Deloitte. *2024 Gen Z and Millennial Survey*. May 2024, www2.deloitte.com/us/en/insights/topics/talent/recruiting-gen-z-and-millennials.html. Accessed 28 Jan. 2025.

Employees want to know that their work contributes to something meaningful. They're looking for leadership that prioritizes impact over ego, collaboration over hierarchy, and sustainability over short-term wins. Companies that invest in purpose-driven cultures not only attract top talent but also retain them. And retention is good business: turnover costs companies millions every year in lost productivity and recruitment expenses.

If you want a committed, innovative workforce, aligning profit with purpose is not optional – it's essential.

3. Society is watching

In the age of social media, businesses are under a microscope. A single misstep – a lack of transparency, unsustainable practices, or ignoring social issues – can spark outrage and damage reputations overnight.

One striking example of this is Starbucks' 2018 racial-bias incident. When two Black men were arrested for sitting in a Philadelphia Starbucks without making a purchase, the event was captured on video and quickly went viral on social media. Outrage spread like wildfire, with consumers condemning Starbucks for what they perceived as racial profiling and a failure to address systemic bias. The backlash was swift and severe, sparking protests, calls for boycotts, and a significant hit to the company's reputation.

Starbucks was forced to respond immediately, closing 8,000 stores nationwide for a day of racial-bias training – a move that reportedly cost the company over $16 million in lost sales. While the company eventually regained public trust by taking responsibility, increasing transparency, and committing to systemic change, the incident underscored a crucial reality: in the age of social media, businesses are under constant scrutiny. A single miscalculation can ignite backlash, undermine trust, and lead to lasting reputational and financial harm if not handled appropriately.

This incident is a cautionary tale for leaders: ignoring societal issues or failing to act with transparency isn't just risky – it's a threat to your brand's survival.

But this societal pressure doesn't have to be thought of as a burden; it can be viewed as a real opportunity. Businesses that take bold action – whether addressing environmental sustainability, advancing diversity, or supporting communities – can become trusted leaders. They're the ones setting the tone, earning goodwill, and building a reputation that endures.

Take Unilever, for example. By embedding sustainability into its core business strategy, it has reduced costs, minimized risks, and grown its portfolio of purpose-driven brands. The result? Brands under Unilever's Sustainable Living Plan grew 69 percent faster than the rest of its business.

Society is calling for businesses to do better – and those that answer the call will reap the rewards.

The Risks of Ignoring This Shift

Let's be clear: clinging to traditional profit-at-all-costs strategies are no longer a safe bet. Businesses that refuse to adapt face three major risks:

1. **Loss of relevance:** customers are moving toward brands that align with their values. Failing to evolve means failing to connect.
2. **Talent drain:** the best employees will leave to find work that matters, costing you money, innovation, and momentum.
3. **Reputation damage:** ignoring societal issues can erode trust, damage brand loyalty, and leave your business vulnerable.

The world is changing, and businesses that don't adapt will struggle to keep up.

Throughout this book, we'll highlight a variety of companies that are leading the way in "net-positivity" – businesses that have successfully aligned profit with purpose and are reaping the benefits.

Some of the most well-known examples include Patagonia, Unilever, and Ben & Jerry's – organizations that have built their brands on sustainability, ethical business practices, and social responsibility. These companies have set the bar high, proving that doing good and doing well aren't mutually exclusive. You'll see them pop up frequently as we explore what it means to lead with purpose.

But they're not the only ones. We'll also investigate the strategies of startups, small businesses, nonprofits, and even government initiatives that are finding innovative ways to embed impact into their operations. From local entrepreneurs to mission-driven organizations, there's no one-size-fits-all approach to net-positivity, and you'll discover plenty of ways to apply these lessons to your own work.

Why does this shift matter?

What's in it for businesses that embrace purpose as a strategic driver?

Let's take a look at the tangible benefits of leading with impact – ones that extend far beyond feel-good branding and into long-term financial and operational success.

The Benefits of Making This Shift

Businesses that embrace purpose as a driver of strategy unlock enormous benefits:

1. **Increased loyalty:** customers who believe in your mission will support you, advocate for you, and stick with you
   - *Example:* Patagonia has built a loyal customer base by prioritizing environmental sustainability, with campaigns such as "Don't Buy This Jacket" encouraging mindful consumption. Their unwavering commitment to purpose has fostered a deeply engaged community and long-term customer loyalty.
2. **Stronger talent:** purpose-driven companies attract and retain employees who are motivated, innovative, and committed.

- *Example:* Unilever, under Paul Polman, integrated sustainability into its core business model. This not only boosted recruitment of top talent but also increased employee engagement, as individuals felt connected to a larger mission of creating a better world.

3. **Resilience:** companies with a long-term, purpose-driven mindset are better equipped to weather challenges and disruptions.
    - *Example:* Starbucks leveraged its purpose-driven mission during economic downturns by maintaining a focus on ethical sourcing, community-building, and employee support. Their College Achievement Plan exemplifies this, fostering loyalty and adaptability among both employees and customers.

4. **Financial growth:** purpose-driven businesses outperform competitors because they deliver value beyond their product or service.
    - *Example:* LEGO invested heavily in sustainability, committing to using eco-friendly materials. This pivot resonated with customers and helped the brand achieve significant growth, proving that purpose and profit can go hand in hand.

The demand for purpose-driven businesses isn't coming – it's already here.

Consumers are demanding it.

Employees are choosing it.

Investors are funding it.

Leaders who embrace this shift now will position their businesses for long-term success and growth.

Those who don't ... risk being left behind.

In the chapters ahead, I'll introduce you to the **Net-Positivity Framework** – a practical, proven approach to aligning profit with purpose. You'll learn how to integrate purpose into your operations, measure impact in meaningful ways, and build a business that thrives financially while making a positive difference.

The world is changing, and businesses that fail to adapt risk more than just financial loss – they risk irrelevance. Consumers are demanding more, employees are seeking purpose, and society is holding businesses accountable like never before.

Here's the challenge for you: will your business rise to the occasion? Will you lead the charge in aligning profit with purpose, creating lasting impact, and inspiring loyalty, innovation, and growth?

The time to act is *now*.

The question is: are you ready to build a business that not only thrives but leaves the world better than you found it?

Let's turn the page and explore what's next.

KEY TAKEAWAYS

The shift

The old "profit-at-all-costs" model no longer works.

Businesses must balance profit with purpose to stay relevant.

- **Consumer and employee demands:** consumers prioritize values, with 73 percent willing to pay more for sustainable products. Employees seek purpose-driven workplaces, rejecting jobs that don't align with their values.

- **Transparency is key:** in today's connected world, businesses are judged by their actions. Purpose builds trust, while inaction damages reputations.

- **The risks of inaction:** ignoring these shifts risks irrelevance, talent loss, and reputation damage.

- **The rewards of purpose:** purpose-driven businesses attract loyalty, retain talent, and outperform competitors.

The Business Case for Balancing Profit and Purpose

I still remember the moment I realized that purpose wasn't just a feel-good concept – it was a business imperative.

It was during my first introductory meeting with a potential new medium-sized business client. I was sitting across from their CEO, who was grappling with declining sales and disengaged employees. He had done everything by the book – cut costs, optimized operations, and ramped up marketing – but nothing was working. Frustrated, he finally admitted, "I don't get it. We're doing everything right, so why aren't people buying?"

That was the problem – he was doing everything right by *old business standards*.

Purpose as a Growth Strategy

The way we define business success is changing. For too long, the bottom line was measured in dollars alone – growth at all costs, profit above all.

But today's business environment demands a broader, more responsible definition of success.

Customers, employees, and investors are no longer just buying products or services – they're buying into what companies stand for. They want to know how you treat your workers, what kind of impact you're making, and whether you're contributing to a better world.

This isn't about politics or posturing. It's about performance. Companies that prioritize both purpose and profit consistently outperform those that don't. Why? Because they build trust, cultivate loyalty, spark innovation, and attract top talent.

The Proof is in the Performance

Let's be clear: leading with purpose is not charity. It's strategy. And it works.

Companies like Salesforce, which has built its brand on ethical tech and community reinvestment, have achieved enormous growth while embedding social responsibility into their business model.

Tesla redefined the automotive industry by making clean energy cool – and valuable.

Allbirds scaled sustainably by making transparency and climate accountability core to its brand.

Cotopaxi, an outdoor gear company, donates a percentage of profits to fight poverty and integrates impact into every level of its operations.

Danone North America became the largest Certified B Corporation in the world, proving that even global giants can thrive while upholding high social and environmental standards.

These companies don't succeed *despite* their commitments to purpose. They succeed *because of them.*

Purpose in Action: Four Different Paths

There is no one-size-fits-all formula for leading with purpose. The most successful companies tailor their approach to fit their values, operations, and customer expectations.

Let's look at the four that have done it well – each in a distinct way:

1. **Unilever made purpose a system-wide mandate.** Through its Sustainable Living Plan, it tied social and environmental goals to business performance across its global portfolio. Brands like Ben & Jerry's and Dove weren't just aligned with purpose – they were built around it. These brands became the company's fastest-growing segments, proving that embedding purpose into supply chains, branding, and innovation pays off.

2. **Patagonia took a more activist approach.** From telling customers not to buy its products to donating partial profits to environmental causes, Patagonia made its values loud and clear. This wasn't just about messaging – it was about operational decisions that reflected a deep commitment to protecting the planet. Their customers responded not just with purchases, but with fierce loyalty.

3. **Greyston Bakery operationalized equity through radical hiring practices.** With its open hiring model – no interviews, no background checks – it created access to jobs for people who have traditionally been shut out. Purpose is embedded not in its products, but in its practices. And that difference has made it a model for inclusive business.

4. **Who Gives a Crap, a cheeky toilet paper brand, built a successful company by tackling a global sanitation crisis.** It donates half its profits to improve sanitation in developing countries and runs a carbon-neutral supply chain. It's a business that proves sustainability, humor, and profitability can coexist – and thrive.

Each of these companies took a different route. What they share is clarity. They know what they stand for, and they've woven that into every business decision. That's the power of real purpose – it doesn't sit on a mission statement; it drives action.

There's no one-size-fits-all model for *what* purpose looks like. But there is a repeatable way to embed it – *how* to structure it so it lives in your culture, operations, and strategy. That's where the **Net-Positivity Framework** comes in.

The framework is built around four essential pillars – guiding principles that help any business, in any industry, bring purpose to life in a measurable, scalable way. Whether your company leads through sustainability, equity, community, or innovation, these pillars ensure that your purpose isn't just inspiring – it's operational.

Why This Matters Now

The risk of inaction is growing. Companies that cling to outdated, profit-only models will lose market share, top talent, and long-term relevance. In contrast, purpose-led businesses are better equipped to navigate economic uncertainty, regulatory changes, and social pressure.

Employees want more than a paycheck – they want meaning. Customers want to buy from brands they trust. Investors are prioritizing ESG (environmental, social, and governance) factors like never before.

Purpose is no longer a differentiator. It's becoming the baseline.

What Comes Next

If you're reading this, you probably already feel the pressure – or the pull – to do things differently. Maybe you've seen the shifting expectations. Maybe you're tired of empty mission statements and want to lead a business that actually lives its values.

Good. That instinct is your competitive advantage.

In the chapters ahead, we'll break down exactly how to build a net-positive business by applying the components of the **Net-Positivity Framework** to drive results, earn loyalty, and leave the world better than we found it. You'll learn how to craft a strategic vision, engage your team, build trust with stakeholders, and turn purpose into measurable progress.

Because purpose and profit aren't opposing forces – they're a flywheel. When you get it right, one fuels the other.

KEY TAKEAWAYS

Purpose drives performance
The old profit-at-all-costs model is fading. Today's most successful companies grow by aligning purpose with profit.

Why it works
- **Customer loyalty:** 87% of consumers prefer brands that reflect their values.
- **Top talent:** Purpose-led companies attract and retain mission-driven employees.
- **Resilience:** Brands thrive in uncertainty by staying rooted in clear values.
- **Investor appeal:** Companies prioritizing ESG draw long-term investment and trust.

Bottom line
Purpose isn't a trend. It's a competitive advantage.

3

Unpacking the Net-Positivity Framework

A few years ago, a former colleague of mine left her corporate job to follow her passion for healthy living and cooking. She poured her heart into opening a vegan café, crafting a menu that was as nourishing as it was delicious. At first, the restaurant thrived – customers loved the food, and her mission resonated. But as time went on, she hit a wall. Rising costs, operational challenges, and the struggle to scale without compromising her values left her exhausted. "I know why I started this," she told me one day, "but I don't know how to make it sustainable."

Her story isn't unique.

So many purpose-driven businesses launch with momentum, only to get stuck when they can't bridge the gap between passion and profitability. That's why having a clear, actionable framework is essential – because purpose alone won't build a thriving business, but the right strategy will.

To build a net-positive business – one that thrives financially while making a meaningful impact – you need more than good intentions. You need a clear, actionable strategy that bridges the gap between your aspirations and the real world. That's where the **Net-Positivity Framework** comes in. This isn't just another business model; it's a blueprint for transforming purpose into profit, ideals into impact, and vision into tangible results.

I've spent years watching businesses struggle to balance their financial goals with their desire to make a difference. Some get stuck in the planning phase, unsure how to move forward. Others dive in but lose momentum when they can't measure their progress or rally their teams around a shared purpose.

The **Net-Positivity Framework** is designed to change that.

Built around *four interconnected pillars*, it offers a roadmap for aligning purpose with profitability and creating businesses that are resilient, sustainable, and wildly successful.

Net-Positivity Framework

STRATEGIC PURPOSE-DRIVEN VISION
Craft a vision that aligns profit with meaningful impact. This defines the purpose and direction of your business.

DATA-DRIVEN MEASUREMENT
Use data to track progress, prove impact and drive decisions.

SUSTAINABLE PURPOSE-DRIVEN OPERATIONS
Align daily practices with core values, integrating sustainability, ethics and efficiency to create meaningful impact.

COLLABORATIVE LEADERSHIP
Empower teams to work together, fostering a culture of purpose and teamwork that drives meaningful change.

Each pillar – Strategic Purpose-Driven Vision; Sustainable Purpose-Driven Operations; Data-Driven Measurement; and Collaborative Leadership – is a piece of the puzzle. Together, they form the foundation of a business that doesn't just survive in today's rapidly changing world – it leads.

In this chapter, I'll give you an overview of these pillars and how they work together to create the kind of business you've always wanted to build.

This is where your journey begins.

Let's dive in and unpack the framework that will transform the way you think about success – because building a net-positive business isn't just the right thing to do; it's the smart thing to do.

The Four Pillars of the Net-Positivity Framework

Pillar 1 – Strategic Purpose-Driven Vision: Defining Your Purpose

Every successful journey begins with a clear destination. For a net-positive business, that destination is a well-defined purpose – one that aligns with your values, drives your mission, and resonates with your stakeholders.

Strategic purpose-driven vision is about identifying what your business stands for and where you want to go. This isn't just about a lofty mission statement; it's about embedding purpose into your long-term goals and ensuring that every decision you make supports them.

Let's look at two companies in the same industry – Kodak and Fujifilm – to illustrate the power of strategic vision.

Kodak, once a titan of the photography industry, had a mission to capture life's memories. While their mission sounded inspiring, it wasn't supported by a forward-looking strategic vision. As digital photography emerged, Kodak clung to its profitable film business, failing to adapt its long-term goals to the industry's rapid transformation. The result? Kodak filed for bankruptcy in 2012, a shadow of its former self, unable to compete in a digital-first world.

Now contrast that with Fujifilm.

Like Kodak, Fujifilm built its business on photography, but its strategic vision went beyond just creating memories – it focused on innovation and adaptability. Fujifilm recognized the shift to digital early and diversified its operations into emerging industries like healthcare and cosmetics, leveraging its expertise in chemicals and imaging technology. Today, Fujifilm remains a thriving company, with significant revenue from industries far beyond photography.

The difference lies in strategic vision.

Kodak had a mission but lacked the vision to evolve.

Fujifilm embedded purpose into its long-term goals and used that vision to guide every decision it made. The lesson is clear: a strong strategic vision isn't just inspiring – it's actionable, adaptable, and the foundation of lasting success.

In the next chapter, we'll explore exactly how you can create a strategic vision that not only inspires but also fuels real, measurable action.

Pillar 2 – Sustainable Purpose-Driven Operations: Aligning Your Processes with Your Mission

Once your vision is clear, it's time to roll up your sleeves and operationalize it. Sustainable purpose-driven operations are where the rubber meets the road – where your big, inspiring ideas actually show up in the day-to-day decisions of your business. This is where you prove that what you say you stand for isn't just a PR stunt or a fancy website slogan.

Imagine walking into a store where every product on the shelf tells a story – one of ethical sourcing, sustainability, and a commitment to the greater good. Now, picture another business where the supply chain is a mystery, operations cut corners, and customers are treated as transactions rather than partners in a shared mission.

The difference?

A company that has taken the time to ask the right questions: do our suppliers and partners reflect our values? Are our internal operations built on sustainability, ethics, and inclusivity? Does our customer experience reinforce our purpose at every touchpoint?

To see what this looks like in action, let's step into the world of businesses that have mastered this process – and a few that have stumbled along the way.

Question 1: are your suppliers and partners aligned with your values?

Ben & Jerry's doesn't just make ice cream – it serves up values by the pint.

The company's supply chain reflects its social and environmental mission, with Fairtrade suppliers, non-GMO ingredients, and dairy farms that prioritize animal welfare. When you're scooping out Cherry Garcia, you're not just satisfying a craving; you're supporting a company that aligns its operations with its purpose.

On the other hand, there's Boohoo, a fast-fashion brand that found itself in hot water when reports surfaced about suppliers exploiting workers. Turns out, customers don't love buying "feel-good" clothes when the backstory involves sweatshop conditions. Boohoo's failure to align its supply chain with ethical standards led to public outrage, proving that cutting corners can cost you more than you save.

Question 2: are your internal operations sustainable, ethical, and inclusive?

Patagonia might as well be the poster child for sustainable purpose-driven operations. From paying employees fair wages to creating a circular economy with its products, the company doesn't just preach sustainability – it lives it. They've built a business that not only thrives but also earns the undying loyalty of customers and employees alike.

Then there's WeWork, which tried to sell itself as the ultimate collaborative, sustainable workspace. Unfortunately, their internal practices didn't match the glossy image. Reports of wasteful spending and questionable leadership made it clear they weren't walking their talk. The fallout was swift, reminding us that you can't fake sustainability and ethics – it must be real, or people will call you out. The rise and fall of WeWork was so monumental that it became the subject of the documentary – *WeWork: Or the Making and Breaking of a $47 Billion Unicorn* – which delves into the company's spectacular rise, its culture of excess, and the leadership failures that led to its downfall.[4]

Question 3: are you embedding purpose into your customer experience?

When it comes to embedding purpose into customer experience, Warby Parker is a shining example. Their "buy-a-pair, give-a-pair" model makes customers feel good about their purchase, knowing they're helping provide glasses to someone in need. Warby Parker is selling more than eyewear – they're selling impact, and it's a strategy that's won them a loyal fanbase.

Volkswagen, on the other hand, drove right into a PR disaster with its "clean-diesel" scandal. Promising environmentally friendly cars while knowingly cheating emissions tests is about as far from aligning purpose with customer experience as you can get. The backlash was fierce, and the damage to consumer trust was monumental. It's a lesson in what happens when your actions don't match your promises.

These examples highlight the power of operationalizing purpose.

---

4   *WeWork: Or the Making and Breaking of a $47 Billion Unicorn.* Directed by Jed Rothstein, Hulu, 2021.

Companies such as Ben & Jerry's, Patagonia, and Warby Parker show how aligning your processes with your mission can build trust, loyalty, and long-term success.

Meanwhile, Boohoo, WeWork, and Volkswagen are cautionary tales of what happens when you fail to walk the talk.

In Chapter 5, we'll explore how to integrate purpose into every corner of your business.

Pillar 3 – Data-Driven Measurement: Proving and Improving Your Impact

Purpose without accountability is more than just wishful thinking – it's a missed opportunity. Without measurable goals and clear tracking, even the most well-intentioned efforts risk being dismissed as empty promises. That's where the third pillar, Data-Driven Measurement, comes into play. This is the engine that keeps your purpose-driven strategies credible, actionable, and impactful.

Imagine a company pledging to reduce its carbon footprint by 50 percent within five years. It's a bold statement, but without measurable data to back it up, it's just that – a statement. Consider IKEA, which set a similar goal and tracked its progress meticulously. By sharing transparent updates, including measurable reductions in carbon emissions, IKEA not only proved its commitment but also gained customer trust and strengthened its brand as a sustainability leader.

This pillar is critical for building trust in a world where people are increasingly skeptical of marketing promises. And don't just take my word for it – a recent study by Edelman found that 88 percent of consumers want brands to be transparent about their sustainability efforts.[5] If you can't back up your claims with data, customers, employees, and

---

5 Edelman. *2019 Edelman Trust Barometer Special Report: In Brands We Trust?* Edelman, 2019, www.edelman.com/sites/g/files/aatuss191/files/2019-06/2019_edelman_trust_barometer_special_report_in_brands_we_trust.pdf. Accessed 28 Jan. 2025.

investors will see through the façade – and they'll take their trust (and dollars) elsewhere.

Data-driven measurement also allows you to refine and improve your strategies. For example, Microsoft publicly tracks its progress toward becoming carbon negative by 2030, using data not only to demonstrate its achievements but also to identify areas for improvement. By consistently reviewing and sharing its metrics, Microsoft stays accountable while continuously innovating to meet its ambitious goals.

From tracking carbon emissions to calculating social return on investment (SROI), data turns your purpose into measurable outcomes. It provides the evidence that your efforts are working, inspires confidence among stakeholders, and gives you the insights you need to improve. Without it, the purpose is just talk. With it, purpose becomes a powerful, trustworthy driver of success.

In Chapter 6, we'll talk about the ways you can measure your own impact, identify the right metrics, and use data to build credibility and drive meaningful change.

Pillar 4 – Collaborative Leadership: Inspiring Teams and Building Partnerships

In the world of business, collaboration isn't just about teams and departments working together – it's the catalyst that elevates an entire mission. A perfect example? The iconic partnership between Shakira and Pepsi. In the early 2000s, Pepsi sought to deepen its connection with younger consumers in Latin America, while Shakira was on the brink of global superstardom. Their collaboration was about more than ads or sponsorships; it was a fusion of culture, music, and branding that propelled both to new heights. Pepsi gained access to a vibrant, engaged audience, and Shakira's fame skyrocketed as she transitioned from a regional sensation to a worldwide icon.

This is the essence of collaborative leadership – strategic partnerships that amplify impact, inspire teams, and create a force greater than the sum of its parts. When businesses adopt this mindset, they don't just grow; they create movements, build lasting relationships, and unlock opportunities that would be impossible alone.

In a net-positive business, leadership isn't about commanding from the top – it's about inspiring others to believe in and work toward a shared vision. Collaborative leadership is the glue that binds purpose-driven strategies together, empowering employees, partners, and stakeholders to contribute their unique strengths toward a common goal.

But why is collaborative leadership so critical?

Because no matter how innovative your ideas or well-defined your strategy, success depends on people. Employees need to feel connected to the work, partners must trust your vision, and stakeholders need to see your commitment in action. A leader who fosters collaboration transforms these groups into a unified force for impact.

Consider Satya Nadella, CEO of Microsoft. When he took the reins in 2014, Microsoft was known for its siloed culture and internal competition. Nadella championed collaboration, transparency, and inclusivity, fostering a growth mindset across the organization.

The result?

A cultural transformation that not only revitalized employee engagement but also positioned Microsoft as a global leader in innovation, sustainability, and purpose-driven business.

Likewise, Jacinda Ardern, former Prime Minister of New Zealand, led with empathy, authenticity, and an unwavering commitment to shared purpose – particularly in times of crisis. Whether addressing climate change or navigating the COVID-19 pandemic, her inclusive leadership style fostered trust, unity, and resilience, earning global recognition for her ability to bring people together around a common mission.

What does collaborative leadership look like in action?

It means:

- **Leading with authenticity and transparency:** leaders like Nadella and Ardern build trust by being open and honest, even in difficult times. They actively listen, acknowledge challenges, and empower others to contribute to solutions.
- **Building cross-sector partnerships to amplify impact:** true collaboration extends beyond an organization's walls. Paul Polman, former CEO of Unilever, understood this when he partnered with competitors, governments, and nonprofits to drive sustainability initiatives. Under his leadership, Unilever set a new standard for purpose-driven business through collective action.
- **Coaching employees to align personal goals with company mission:** when employees see their work as part of something bigger, they're more engaged, innovative, and motivated. Howard Schultz, former CEO of Starbucks, embodied this by investing in employee development and creating programs that empowered baristas to feel integral to the company's mission.

Collaborative leadership isn't about issuing directives from above – it's about creating a culture where every voice is heard, every contribution is valued, and every stakeholder is invested in the mission. When leaders embrace collaboration, they unlock the full potential of their teams and build partnerships that extend their impact far beyond their organization.

In Chapter 7, we'll explore how you can embrace collaborative leadership to inspire your people, align your partnerships, and create a purpose-driven culture that thrives on shared success. Because in a net-positive business, leadership isn't just a position – it's a movement.

Purpose-driven operations aren't just a nice-to-have; they're your proof of concept. They show your customers, employees, and stakeholders that you're not just serious about your mission – you're living it.

And that's how you turn a vision into a thriving reality.

What we've done so far in this book is lay the foundation.

We've explored the concept of net-positivity and why it matters in today's business landscape. You now understand the four pillars of the **Net-Positivity Framework** and the importance of aligning your operations with your mission. But understanding the "why" is only the beginning.

In the chapters ahead, we're going to dive into the "how."

Each of the four pillars – Strategic Purpose-Driven Vision; Sustainable Purpose-Driven Operations; Data-Driven Measurement; and Collaborative Leadership – will be explored in greater detail.

You'll gain actionable strategies, practical tools, and real-world examples that empower you to integrate these concepts seamlessly into your business.

By doing so, you'll cultivate stronger relationships with values-aligned partners, create a workplace culture that attracts and retains top talent, and design customer experiences that inspire loyalty and advocacy.

As a result, your business will thrive with purpose, stand out in a crowded market, and drive meaningful impact that resonates with both your customers and your bottom line.

Imagine a business where every decision – every product launched, every partnership formed, every customer interaction – is guided by a clear, unwavering sense of purpose. A business that doesn't just compete in the marketplace but redefines it. Picture a company where employees feel deeply connected to their work, where customers aren't just buyers but advocates, and where profits grow in tandem with positive impact.

With the **Net-Positive Framework**, success isn't measured solely in numbers but in the lasting change your business creates – an industry transformed, a community engaged, and a ripple effect that extends far beyond your bottom line. This is more than a strategy; it's the foundation for a business that leaves the world better than it found it.

Now it's time to roll up your sleeves and get to work.

Whether it's crafting a vision that inspires, embedding purpose into your daily operations, measuring your impact, or leading with authenticity and collaboration, the chapters ahead will give you the tools you need to make it happen.

This is your roadmap to building a resilient, purpose-driven business that thrives financially while making a meaningful difference.

> **KEY TAKEAWAYS**
>
> **Purpose with strategy**
>
> Net-positivity is an actionable framework for balancing profit with meaningful impact.
>
> **The Four Pillars of Net-Positivity**
>
> 1. **Strategic purpose-driven vision:** define a clear, inspiring, and forward-looking purpose to guide decisions and long-term goals.
> 2. **Sustainable purpose-driven operations:** align daily processes – such as supply chains, hiring practices, and customer experiences – with your mission.
> 3. **Data-driven measurement:** track and share progress transparently to build trust, prove impact, and refine strategies.
> 4. **Collaborative leadership:** inspire and empower employees, partners, and stakeholders to unite behind your mission.

PART II
THE HOW

Building the Foundation

Now that you understand the power of a net-positive business, it's time to build the foundation to make it real. Part II: The How – Building the Foundation takes you step-by-step through defining your purpose, aligning operations with impact, measuring what matters, and leading with collaboration. These chapters (4–7) will equip you with the strategies, tools, and the leadership mindset needed to turn purpose into action and create lasting change.

Pillar 1: Strategic Purpose-Driven Vision
Defining Your Purpose

STRATEGIC PURPOSE-DRIVEN VISION
Craft a vision that aligns profit with meaningful impact. This defines the purpose and direction of your business.

A 2019 study by Deloitte found that purpose-driven companies grow three times faster than their competitors, yet only 27 percent of businesses say they have a clearly articulated and operationalized purpose.[6] The disconnect isn't due to a lack of ambition – most leaders *want* their

---

6 Deloitte. *Purpose-Driven Companies Evolve Faster than Their Competitors*. Deloitte Insights, 2019, www2.deloitte.com/us/en/insights/topics/marketing-and-sales-operations/global-marketing-trends/2020/purpose-driven-companies.html. Accessed 30 Jan. 2025.

businesses to stand for something meaningful. The challenge is defining that purpose in a way that guides strategy, decision-making, and long-term success.

I once worked with a business owner who had built a successful company but felt like something was missing. "I know we make great products, and I know we're profitable,' he told me. 'But at the end of the day, what's the actual point? We keep growing, we keep selling … but for what? Just to make more money? It feels like something is missing, like success shouldn't feel this empty."

That realization sparked a turning point.

He and his leadership team spent months digging deep – reflecting on their values, their impact, and the real change they wanted to create. When they finally defined their purpose – helping people live more sustainably through everyday products – the shift was immediate. Employees felt more engaged, customers connected more deeply, and the company's growth accelerated.

Defining your business purpose isn't just a branding exercise – it's the foundation for sustainable success.

In this chapter, we'll walk through how to uncover, articulate, and embed your purpose so that it fuels everything from your strategy to your culture. Because when you know exactly *why* your business exists, you unlock a competitive advantage that no competitor can replicate.

In the previous chapters, we explored the **Net-Positivity Framework** – what it is, why it matters, and why the traditional "profit-at-all-costs" model is as outdated as dial-up internet. We've laid the groundwork, highlighting the power of purpose-driven strategies and showing you that aligning profit with impact isn't just a good idea – it's the only idea, if you want to thrive in today's world.

Now comes the exciting part: figuring out how to implement this in your business or organization.

It's one thing to understand the concept of balancing profit and purpose; it's another to make it happen.

This chapter is where the rubber meets the road, where your lofty aspirations start to take shape as actionable steps.

Let me warn you upfront: this part of the journey will challenge you to dig deep. It's like spring cleaning for your business – unearthing what you stand for, tossing out what doesn't fit, and building a foundation that reflects your true purpose. But unlike spring-cleaning, this work is a lot more fun (and there's no endlessly mismatched collection of USB cables and random chargers to sort through).

Here, we're going to focus on the heart of your business: your purpose.

It's not just your mission statement or your company values slapped on a website. Purpose is your "why" – your reason for existing beyond the bottom line. It's what gets you out of bed in the morning – and it's what keeps your customers, employees, and partners loyal to you when things get tough.

By the end of this chapter, you'll not only know how to craft a purpose that's clear, inspiring, and actionable, but you'll also see how it can guide every decision you make.

So, grab your notebook (or a good mental checklist), and let's get started on defining your "why."

This is where the magic begins – where your business transforms from "just another company" into a force for good in the world.

Why Purpose Matters

Think of purpose as the soul of your business – the heartbeat that gives it life beyond the numbers. It's what makes your organization more than just a profit machine. Purpose attracts customers who share your values, inspires employees to go above and beyond, and it builds trust with investors and partners who want to back something meaningful.

When my partner and I started Hera Associates, we didn't want to just start a consulting firm – we set out to build a *movement*.

We knew that businesses and governments had the potential to drive real social and economic impact, but too often, outdated systems and short-term thinking got in the way. We saw an opportunity to do things differently – to create a business that wasn't just about advising others but about setting a new standard for how organizations operate, proving that purpose and profit are not only compatible but mutually reinforcing.

From day one, we committed to building Hera Associates on values, determination, and a relentless passion for delivering real, transformative results. We believed that by instilling impact into every layer of business operations, companies could achieve stronger financial outcomes, retain top talent, and create lasting value for their stakeholders and communities. More importantly, we believed that taking care of people – our employees, our partners, and the communities we serve – was not just the right thing to do, but the *smartest business strategy*.

This belief shaped everything we built. It's why we landed on our mission: to transform and elevate business to create net-positive social and economic significance for the long-term, so everyone, everywhere can thrive.

And our vision: an inclusive and equitable world where everyone has equal opportunity to achieve, succeed, and positively contribute to a vibrant community.

By building net-positive businesses that change the world, and elevating purpose-driven leaders and organizations to success, we are proving that the future of business is not just about maximizing profit – it's about creating *lasting impact*.

This is the model we want to help others build.

We know it's possible because we've done it ourselves.

And through the **Net-Positivity Framework**, you'll have the tools to do the same.

Let's look at some bigger companies that you're likely familiar with.

Take LEGO, for example. Their purpose – "inspire and develop the builders of tomorrow" – is more than a tagline; it's embedded into everything they do. This purpose drives their commitment to sustainability, such as producing bricks made from plant-based or recycled materials, and their investment in education, such as developing play-based learning tools for classrooms.

But what makes LEGO's purpose especially powerful is how it connects with its customers. Parents and educators don't just buy LEGO sets because they're fun (though they are); they buy them because LEGO's mission resonates with their own values: creativity, learning, and sustainability. By aligning their business goals with societal impact, LEGO has not only built a loyal customer base but also established itself as a leader in creativity, innovation, and corporate responsibility.

For you, the takeaway is clear: a strong purpose has the power to differentiate your business in ways that products or pricing alone cannot. It becomes a magnet for like-minded customers, a rallying cry for your employees, and a foundation for long-term growth.

As you define your own purpose, think about what your business truly stands for and how you can connect that to the broader needs and aspirations of the people you serve. After all, purpose isn't just good for the soul of your business – it's good for business, period.

Crafting a purpose as impactful as LEGO's might seem daunting, but it doesn't have to be. To make this process easier, we've created the *Net-Positivity Framework Toolkit*, a step-by-step guide designed to help you reflect on your "why" and connect it to the broader societal goals that matter most to your stakeholders. This toolkit, available as a free download with this book, provides templates, prompts, and practical exercises to guide you through each step. Whether you're a seasoned leader or just beginning to align your business with impact, the *Net-Positivity Framework Toolkit* will help you turn reflection into action.

In the meantime, I've outlined the steps to define your purpose below.

Steps to Defining Your Purpose

Step 1: Reflect on Your "Why"

Every great purpose starts with a question: why does your business exist? Reflecting on your "why" helps you uncover the core reason for your company's existence – beyond profit margins or operational goals. Was it to solve a specific problem? Meet an unmet need? Change the world in a meaningful way?

Take Airbnb as an example.

Their purpose – "to create a world where anyone can belong anywhere" – emerged from a simple yet powerful idea: helping people find affordable lodging while fostering cultural connection and community. By identifying this "why," Airbnb shaped a purpose that resonates deeply with both guests and hosts, creating a strong foundation for their business strategy.

Action Steps

Gather your leadership team or key stakeholders for a brainstorming session. Create a safe space for open dialogue and focus on the following three questions. Here's how businesses, nonprofits, and government organizations might answer them:

1. **What problem are we solving?**
   - *Business example:* a renewable energy startup might answer, "We're addressing the global reliance on fossil fuels and the need for accessible, affordable clean-energy solutions."
   - *Nonprofit example:* a food bank could say, "We're solving the problem of food insecurity in underserved communities by redistributing surplus food to those who need it most."
   - *Government organization example:* a city transportation department might identify, "We're solving the challenge of traffic congestion and the environmental impact of urban transportation."

2. **Who benefits from our work, and how?**
   - *Business example:* a fitness app company might say, "Our users benefit by gaining access to affordable, personalized fitness plans that help them lead healthier lives."
   - *Nonprofit example:* an organization focused on youth mentorship might answer, "Underserved students benefit from our work by gaining access to resources, guidance, and opportunities that prepare them for college and careers."
   - *Government organization example:* a public health agency could respond, "Local residents benefit through improved access to preventative care, leading to healthier communities and reduced healthcare costs."

3. **What legacy do we want to leave behind?**
   - *Business example:* a sustainable fashion brand might say, "We want to leave behind a world where fashion is circular and no longer contributes to environmental degradation."

- *Nonprofit example:* a wildlife conservation nonprofit might answer, "Our legacy is a thriving ecosystem where endangered species are protected and preserved for future generations."
- *Government organization example:* a city-planning office might declare, "We want to leave behind an urban environment that is sustainable, livable, and inclusive for all citizens."

This reflective process helps clarify your organization's purpose and ties it to real-world impact. Once you've answered these questions, look for common themes that emerge. These will form the foundation of your purpose statement, guiding everything from your operations to your partnerships and long-term strategy.

Remember: purpose isn't static – it evolves as your organization grows and as societal needs shift. The key is to start with a strong "why" and let it guide you through the journey ahead.

In the next step, we'll explore how to connect your purpose to broader societal goals, making your mission even more powerful and relevant.

Step 2: Connect Your Purpose to Broader Societal Goals

Your purpose doesn't exist in a vacuum – it's part of a bigger story. It connects to the societal, environmental, and economic challenges shaping our world today. By aligning your purpose with an established global framework, you can amplify your impact and show that your business is actively contributing to something much larger than itself.

One of the most comprehensive frameworks to consider is the United Nations' Sustainable Development Goals (SDGs). I'll admit, I don't always love everything about the UN – it's a massive institution with its fair share of bureaucracy – but the SDGs? Those I love.

Why?

Because they're practical, clear, and universally relevant. They break down some of the world's biggest challenges – poverty, inequality, and climate change – into 17 actionable goals. They give businesses like yours and mine a way to connect purpose to measurable progress.

For example: If your company focuses on renewable energy, you might align with SDG 7: Affordable and Clean Energy, working to expand access to sustainable power. If you're in fashion, SDG 12: Responsible Consumption and Production could guide you toward minimizing waste and adopting ethical sourcing.

But the SDGs aren't the only game in town.

There are other frameworks that might better suit your specific mission or industry, and we'll explore a few of those, too:

- **B Corporation Certification Framework (B Corp)**

    Why I like it: the B Corp framework offers a rigorous way to measure your entire social and environmental performance. It's like the ultimate stamp of approval for businesses that want to prove they're walking the talk.

- **Global Reporting Initiative (GRI)**

    Why I like it: the GRI is great for businesses that want to get serious about transparency. It focuses on sustainability reporting, giving you a way to track and communicate your environmental, social, and governance (ESG) efforts.

- **Doughnut Economics Framework**

    Why I like it: it's bold and visual. This framework challenges businesses to balance human well-being (the social foundation) with environmental limits (the ecological ceiling).

- **Corporate Social Responsibility (CSR) Guidelines**

    Why I like it: CSR is flexible and easy to adapt to your specific goals. It's perfect if you're just starting to incorporate purpose-driven strategies.

- **Impact Genome Project**
  Why I like it: it brings a data-driven, evidence-based approach to measuring social impact. The Impact Genome Project creates standardized "genomes" for different social outcomes – whether it's economic mobility, education, or sustainability – allowing businesses and nonprofits to quantify and benchmark their impact in a way that aligns with funders, investors, and stakeholders.

With these frameworks in mind, the next step is to determine which one aligns best with your organization's mission and goals and to begin mapping your purpose to a specific, actionable strategy.

Action Step 1: Choose Your Framework
Ask key questions:

- Which global challenges does my business address?
- How do my current activities align with these challenges?
- What additional areas could I focus on to amplify my impact?

Action Step 2: Map Your Purpose to a Goal
- For instance: a small business in renewable energy might map its purpose to SDG 7: Affordable and Clean Energy, focusing on expanding access to off-grid power solutions.
- A nonprofit tackling food insecurity might align with B Corp's Community Standards, ensuring its work uplifts local economies and marginalized groups.

Action Step 3: Define Specific Contributions
Break it down. What can your business do to support these goals? For example:

- "We'll reduce our carbon footprint by 30 percent over the next five years."
- "We'll donate ten percent of profits to local educational initiatives."

Action Step 4: Share Your Alignment

Once you've identified your framework and goals, talk about them! Share your alignment in your mission statement, marketing materials, and stakeholder updates. This isn't about bragging – it's about transparency and trust.

The right framework transforms your purpose from an abstract idea into something tangible and credible. Whether you use the SDGs, B Corp standards, or another approach, aligning with a global or industry-specific framework makes your mission more impactful and your strategy more focused.

Next, we'll move from the "why" to the "what", by exploring how to turn this alignment into a clear and inspiring purpose statement that serves as the compass for your entire organization.

Let's take your purpose to the next level.

Step 3: Define a Clear and Inspiring Statement

Your purpose statement is more than a collection of words – it's your business's heartbeat, the rallying cry that inspires your team, customers, and partners. It should be clear, concise, and inspiring – specific enough to guide decision-making but flexible enough to grow with your business.

Think of it as your North Star.

When challenges arise or decisions get murky – like when everyone on your team has an opinion about the "right" way to move forward – your purpose statement will keep you grounded and focused on what matters most.

Here are a couple of example Purpose Statements to drive the idea home:

- **Microsoft:** "To empower every person and every organization on the planet to achieve more."
- **Tesla:** "To accelerate the world's transition to sustainable energy."

Now, I know what you might be thinking: *not everyone's a fan of Elon Musk or Microsoft's way of doing things.*

Fair enough. Whether you're inspired by Tesla's bold goals, skeptical of Microsoft's reach, or just here to figure out how to make your own mark, these statements still serve as great examples of clear, inspiring purpose.

Here are examples from a small business and nonprofit to demonstrate that you don't have to be the big powerhouse like Microsoft or Tesla to have purpose:

- **Small business example:** Kerb, a company operating food halls and supporting independent food traders, refined their mission statement: "To be the most impactful hospitality company in the world."
- **Nonprofit example:** Elias Fund, a United States-based nonprofit organization, focuses on community development and education in Zimbabwe. Their mission is: "Spreading hope and opportunity in Zimbabwe through indigenous empowerment, and engaging the current youth culture of the United States by encouraging a positive identity centered on social justice."

These statements are simple yet profound. They capture the "why" behind the organization's work while inspiring people to rally around their mission.

Let's examine how to craft a statement like this for your business – one that feels authentic and uniquely yours.

We're going to break this down into manageable steps, and to make it relatable, we'll consider a fictional company called GreenSprout, which provides sustainable packaging solutions.

1. **Start with reflection**
   Gather your team and revisit the questions you answered in Step 1:
   - What problem are we solving?
   - Who benefits from our work, and how?
   - What legacy do we want to leave behind?

For our fictional company, GreenSprout, the answers might look like this:
- *Problem:* reducing single-use plastic waste in packaging.
- *Who benefits:* consumers and businesses looking for eco-friendly packaging alternatives, as well as the planet itself.
- *Legacy:* a future where sustainable packaging is the norm, not the exception.

2. **Identify key themes**
   From your reflection, pull out key themes. For GreenSprout, the key themes might include:
   - Sustainability and environmental stewardship.
   - Innovation in packaging solutions.
   - Empowering businesses to make eco-friendly choices.

   These themes will form the foundation of your purpose statement.

3. **Draft a statement**
   Turn those themes into a concise, inspiring statement. Start with a rough draft – it doesn't need to be perfect. For GreenSprout, the first draft might be:

   "To reduce single-use plastics by providing sustainable, innovative packaging solutions for businesses worldwide."

4. **Refine and simplify**
   Great purpose statements are both impactful and easy to remember. Work on simplifying your draft while keeping the essence intact. After some refinement, GreenSprout's purpose statement could become:

   "To revolutionize packaging with sustainable solutions that protect the planet and empower businesses."

5. **Test your statement**
   Share your draft with your team, customers, or stakeholders. Ask for feedback:
   - Does it resonate?
   - Does it reflect your mission and values?
   - Does it inspire action?

For GreenSprout, feedback might reveal that "revolutionize" feels too aggressive, so they revise it to:

"To lead the shift to sustainable packaging, protecting the planet and empowering businesses."

Your purpose statement will guide your business's journey. It's the filter for every decision you make, from product development to partnerships. It also connects with people – your team, customers, and community – on a deeper level, creating a sense of shared mission and belonging.

By the end of this step, you should have a purpose statement that feels authentic, powerful, and actionable. It's not just a slogan; it's a promise.

And in the next step, we'll explore how to embed that promise into your daily operations, ensuring it's lived out at every level of your business.

Step 4: Use Purpose to Guide Decision-Making

Your purpose is more than a set of inspiring words – it's a decision-making compass that helps you navigate the complexities of running a business. Whether you're evaluating new partnerships, launching a product, or responding to challenges, your purpose provides clarity and direction. It ensures that every choice you make, big or small, supports your mission and reinforces your values. When faced with tough decisions, a purpose filter helps you answer the critical question: does this move us closer to the impact we want to make?

Consider Patagonia again.

Their purpose – protecting the planet – guides everything they do, from donating one percent of sales to environmental causes to taking bold political stances. These decisions aren't made on a whim; they're intentional moves aligned with their mission. It's why customers trust them, employees stay loyal, and their business thrives.

Let's take this idea and make it actionable for you. I know decision-making isn't always easy – it can feel like a balancing act on a tightrope of competing priorities. That's where a purpose filter comes in. Let's create one for our fictional company, GreenSprout, and assess how you can use it for your own business.

How to Create a Purpose Filter for Decision-Making

A purpose filter is essentially a checklist or set of guiding questions that ensures every decision supports your mission. For GreenSprout, whose purpose is "To lead the shift to sustainable packaging, protecting the planet and empowering businesses," the filter might look something like this:

1. **Does this align with our sustainability goals?**
   - *Example question:* does this decision help reduce environmental impact, either directly or indirectly?
   - *Scenario:* if GreenSprout is considering using a new material for their packaging, they'd ask: is this material recyclable, compostable, or otherwise eco-friendly? If it's not, it's a no-go.

2. **Does this empower businesses to make better environmental choices?**
   - *Example question:* does this help our customers transition to more sustainable practices?
   - *Scenario:* GreenSprout is deciding whether to invest in an educational campaign for clients. They'd ask: does this help businesses understand the value of sustainable packaging? If yes, it aligns with their purpose.

3. **Is this decision financially responsible while staying true to our mission?**
   - *Example question:* does this balance sustainability with profitability?
   - *Scenario:* if GreenSprout is looking at a supplier offering a cheaper, non-sustainable option, the filter would kick in: does this compromise our purpose? If it does, they'd opt for the sustainable supplier, even if it costs more upfront.

4. **Does this align with our brand values and build trust?**
   - *Example question:* how will this decision impact our reputation with customers, employees, and stakeholders?
   - *Scenario:* if GreenSprout considers partnering with a supplier that has questionable environmental practices, they'd ask: would this erode customer trust? If the answer is yes, they'd look elsewhere.
5. **Does this reflect the long-term legacy we want to create?**
   - *Example question:* is this a decision we'll be proud of in ten years?
   - *Scenario:* GreenSprout is deciding whether to prioritize short-term profits over long-term sustainability goals. The filter would help them choose the path that supports their vision for lasting impact.

Here's the key: you don't have to create the perfect checklist on day one. Start with a simple set of questions like the ones above and refine them over time. Share your purpose filter with your team, encourage them to use it in their own decision-making, and revisit it regularly to make sure it still aligns with your goals.

I'll be honest – there will be moments when your purpose filter challenges you to make harder (and sometimes more expensive) decisions. But those are the moments when your purpose shines the brightest. Staying true to your mission, even when it's inconvenient, builds trust, loyalty, and long-term success.

Action Steps
- Draft your own purpose filter, with three to five guiding questions that align with your mission.
- Use it for at least one major decision in the coming month, and then reflect on how it influenced the outcome.

Share it with your team and encourage feedback to refine it further. Purpose-driven decision-making keeps your business authentic and focused. It ensures that every choice you make, from the suppliers you work with to the strategies you implement, reflects your mission and strengthens your impact.

Step 5: Embed Purpose into Your Culture

Your purpose won't create change if it's confined to a slide deck or a motivational poster. For it to truly matter, your purpose needs to live in the DNA of your organization – it must be felt in the way people work, collaborate, and show up every day. Purpose becomes real when it's infused into your culture, shaping not just what you do, but why you do it.

Let's get real for a second: if your team doesn't believe in your purpose or see how it connects to their daily work, it's not going to stick. This step is about making purpose something that inspires and energizes everyone, from your newest hire to your most seasoned leader.

Think about Salesforce and their 1-1-1 model. They dedicate one percent of equity, one percent of product, and one percent of employee time to philanthropy. This isn't just a nice-to-have – it's baked into the culture. Employees know they're part of something bigger than the bottom line, and that connection fosters loyalty, innovation, and pride in the workplace.

But this isn't just for tech giants like Salesforce. No matter your size or industry, incorporating purpose into your culture is the key to unlocking the full potential of your team – and creating an organization people are proud to be part of.

Here's how you can bring your purpose to life in your organization, with a sample process to make it feel actionable and relatable:

1. **Start with storytelling**

    Purpose comes alive when it's connected to real stories that resonate. Share the "why" behind your purpose with your team.
    - *Example:* at GreenSprout, the leadership team kicks off every onboarding session with the story of how the company started –

born from a desire to fight single-use plastics after the founders saw firsthand the devastating effects of pollution on a beach cleanup trip.
- *Action tip:* incorporate these origin stories into team meetings, newsletters, and training sessions. Let people see the human side of your mission.

2. **Weave purpose into onboarding**

   Your team's first impression matters. Make sure every new hire understands your purpose and how it connects to their role.
   - *Example:* GreenSprout's onboarding includes a hands-on session where new employees create a sustainability pledge, outlining how they'll contribute to the company's mission in their daily work
   - *Action tip:* go beyond a PowerPoint presentation. Create interactive sessions that encourage team members to reflect on how their role supports the mission.

3. **Make purpose a priority in daily operations**

   Purpose shouldn't just show up in annual reports; it should be part of everyday decisions and interactions.
   - *Example:* GreenSprout incorporates purpose into their team meetings by dedicating time to discuss how recent decisions align with their sustainability goals. Wins – big and small – are celebrated, like signing a partnership with a zero-waste supplier or reducing office waste.
   - *Action tip:* dedicate a portion of team meetings to reflect on how your purpose is being fulfilled. Share examples and celebrate progress.

4. **Celebrate successes**

   When your purpose comes to life, recognize it – and make sure your team knows they're part of that success.

- *Example:* GreenSprout holds a quarterly "Purpose in Action" spotlight where employees nominate colleagues who have gone above and beyond to support the mission. Winners receive a donation made in their name to an environmental nonprofit.
- *Action tip:* share success stories widely, both internally and externally. Make purpose-driven achievements a point of pride.

5. **Align incentives with purpose**

    Purpose shouldn't feel like extra work – it should feel rewarding. Align incentives and recognition with your mission to create buy-in across all levels.
    - *Example:* GreenSprout ties bonuses to sustainability KPIs, such as reducing waste or hitting carbon-neutral milestones, showing employees that purpose-driven success is a priority.
    - *Action tip:* create incentives tied to purpose, whether through recognition programs, bonuses, or public shout-outs.

Embedding purpose into your culture isn't just good for your team – it's good for your business. A strong culture of purpose drives employee engagement, attracts top talent, and builds loyalty among customers and partners. People want to work for and with organizations that stand for something meaningful.

As you move forward, remember that embedding purpose into your culture isn't a one-time project – it's a continuous process that grows stronger the more you live it, share it, and celebrate it. Purpose becomes truly transformative when it's woven into the fabric of your daily operations.

In the next chapter, we'll dive into how to bring your purpose to life through the systems, processes, and decisions that drive your business every day. You'll learn how to align your operations with your mission, ensuring that every action your organization takes reflects your values and amplifies your impact.

KEY TAKEAWAYS

Purpose is your "why"

It's the soul of your business, driving loyalty, trust, and long-term success by aligning your goals with societal impact.

- Reflect and refine.
- Connect to bigger goals.
- Craft a clear purpose statement.
- Embed purpose into your culture.

5

Pillar 2: Sustainable Purpose-Driven Operations

Aligning Your Processes with Your Mission

SUSTAINABLE PURPOSE-DRIVEN OPERATIONS
Align daily practices with core values, integrating sustainability, ethics and efficiency to create meaningful impact.

Ninety percent of executives believe their company has a clear purpose, but only 46 percent of employees agree.

And yes, that is awkward!

It's like a restaurant claiming to be a five-star dining experience while the servers are still trying to figure out what's on the menu.

Purpose isn't just a statement on your website – it must be embedded into the daily operations of your business. Otherwise, it's just another corporate buzzword floating in the void, right next to "synergy" and "low-hanging fruit."

This chapter is about turning your well-defined purpose into something real – something that your employees, customers, and partners can see, feel, and experience in every interaction with your business. Because if purpose is your mission, then operationalizing it is how you make it matter.

By now, you've done the soul-searching. You've defined your purpose, crafted a vision that goes beyond profit, and connected your "why" to broader societal goals.

It's time to take it a step further.

Welcome to the "how" of purpose-driven business – the part where you take those lofty ideals and weave them into the day-to-day fabric of your operations.

This is where purpose comes alive. It's not just a slogan or a statement tucked into your annual report – it's the decisions you make, the processes you build, and the way your business shows up in the world. And trust me, this is where the magic happens.

Think of it like baking a cake (stay with me here). Your purpose is the recipe – clear, inspiring, and grounded in why you're baking in the first place. But sustainable purpose-driven operations? That's the mixing, measuring, and baking. It's where the ingredients come together to create something real, something that everyone can taste and enjoy. Let's make sure your cake rises … and doesn't fall flat like a forgotten soufflé.

Your operations are where the rubber meets the road. They're how you prove your purpose is more than talk, and you demonstrate to your customers, employees, and stakeholders that you're walking the walk.

I know this sentiment might sound repetitive – I've said it before in previous chapters, and I'm saying it again now.

Why?

Because it bears repeating. This idea is the heartbeat of the entire book: your operations are where purpose meets action, and it's through this alignment that businesses truly thrive. Sustainable purpose-driven operations aren't just a nice-to-have; they're how you prove your mission isn't just words on a page. They build trust, drive measurable outcomes, and create a ripple effect of impact – higher efficiency, loyal customers, reduced costs, and meaningful contributions to society.

This repetition isn't accidental. It's intentional because this principle is the cornerstone of balancing profit with meaningful, transformative purpose. It's the "why" behind everything we've talked about and everything you're about to learn. My mission is to make sure business leaders like you not only grasp the importance of this balance but also feel empowered to make it happen in a way that delivers the profit, prestige, and lifestyle you want for yourself and your team.

Companies that Balance Purpose and Profit

Let's look at how some companies are nailing this balance between purpose and profit in their operations:

- IKEA has woven sustainability into its DNA by committing to use only renewable or recycled materials in all its products by 2030. It's not just a goal – it's a roadmap for transforming its supply chain and production processes, from sourcing sustainable wood to designing products that can be reused or recycled.
- Allbirds doesn't just make comfy shoes; it's reimagining how products are made. By using sustainable materials like wool and sugarcane and offsetting their carbon emissions, they're proving you can be stylish, innovative, and environmentally conscious all at once.

- Starbucks extends its purpose into local communities through initiatives like the "FoodShare" program, which repurposes unsold food to combat waste and hunger, and career-development programs that provide employees with education and training. These efforts show that a sustainable purpose-driven operation doesn't stop at the product – it's implanted in the way a company interacts with people and the planet.

Are these companies perfect?

Of course not. No business is.

If you find one that is, let me know so I can ask them how they handle meetings that could've been emails. But seriously, perfection isn't the point – it's progress. These companies are taking bold, meaningful steps to align their operations with their purpose, and it's paying off in real ways: stronger customer loyalty, a reputation for innovation, and measurable impact that resonates with stakeholders.

Let's revisit IKEA.

Their sustainability commitment isn't just a promise; it's showing results. By 2022, they had already switched over 98 percent of their wood to FSC-certified or recycled sources, and they're making strides toward circular design practices. Customers appreciate not only the affordable furniture, but the fact that it doesn't cost the planet nearly as much as it used to.

And Allbirds.

Since launching, the company has been transparent about its carbon footprint, cutting it down by 12 percent per product and offsetting what remains to achieve net-zero carbon emissions. They've built a cult-following, not just for their cloud-like shoes but for their commitment to sustainability – a quality that makes people feel good about their purchase, not just their feet.

And finally, Starbucks, whose FoodShare program has redistributed millions of meals to food banks across the United States, reducing waste while addressing food insecurity. Add to that their investment in career pathways for employees – like the Starbucks College Achievement Plan, which has helped over 20,000 employees graduate – and you see a company doubling down on purpose in ways that matter to its people and communities.

None of these companies claim to have all the answers, but their results show what happens when businesses prioritize purpose: customers stick around, employees stay engaged, and communities feel the impact. That's not just good business – it's meaningful business.

So, what's stopping you from taking the first step?

Aligning your operations with your purpose might feel like a big leap, but it's entirely doable when you break it down into manageable steps.

Let's dive into how you can start embedding purpose into your daily practices – one step at a time.

Steps to Align Purpose with Profit

Step 1: Conduct a Sustainability Audit

Before you can align your operations with your purpose, you need a clear understanding of your current practices. A sustainability audit is like a diagnostic check-up for your business – it identifies what's working, what's not, and where there's room for improvement. It's your starting point for embedding purpose into daily operations.

A sustainability audit evaluates your organization's inputs (what you bring in), processes (how you operate), and outputs (what you produce or impact). It looks at everything from energy consumption and material sourcing to waste production and community contributions. Think of it as the Marie Kondo of business operations – does this spark sustainable

Chapter 5: Purpose-Driven Operations – Embedding Impact Into Daily Practices – Toolkit

This interactive toolkit Is designed to help you embed your purpose into daily operations. Whether you're running a business, nonprofit or government agency, these resources will guide you through practical steps to align your operations with your mission, creating measurable impact along the way.

Step 1: Conduct a Sustainability Audit

What to Do:

Use this worksheet to assess your inputs, processes, and outputs. Identify areas of alignment with your purpose and opportunities for improvement.

Sustainability Audit Worksheet

Category	Questions	Current Practices	Opportunities for Improvement
Inputs	Are our raw materials sourced sustainably and ethically?	Example: Recycled materials for packaging	Example: Partner with Fair Trade Certified vendors
	Are suppliers adhering to our values and standards?	Example: Local suppliers	Example: Audit supplier practices
	Is our energy use efficient and renewable?	Example: LED lighting	Example: Transition to solar power
Processes	Are production methods optimized for efficiency and sustainability?	Example: Minimal packaging	Example: Shift to biodegradable options
	Are we managing waste responsibly (reduce, reuse, recycle)?	Example: Recycling program	Example: Introduce composting
	Are logistics optimized to minimize carbon emissions?	Example: Efficient routing	Example: Adopt electric vehicles

Image 1.1: Sustainability Audit from The Net-Positivity Framework Toolkit

joy, or is it time to toss it? It's an honest inventory of how aligned your actions are with your purpose.

- **Evaluate your inputs**

    Start by looking at everything your business brings in – raw materials, energy, and suppliers. Are they aligned with your purpose and values?

    Key questions to ask:
    - Are your raw materials sourced sustainably and ethically?
    - Are your suppliers following environmental, labor, and ethical standards?
    - Is your energy coming from renewable sources, or are you relying on fossil fuels?

    Examples:
    - *Food company:* a food brand might review whether its produce is certified organic or Fair Trade, ensuring fair wages and safe working conditions for farmers.
    - *Nonprofit:* a nonprofit distributing medical supplies might assess whether its partners meet ethical standards in manufacturing.
    - *Government organization:* a city government might analyze its procurement practices to ensure its sourcing energy-efficient technologies or eco-friendly office supplies.

- **Assess your processes**

    Next, examine how your business operates. This includes production methods, waste management, and logistics.

    Key questions to ask:
    - Are your production processes as efficient and sustainable as possible?
    - How much waste are you generating, and can it be reduced, reused, or recycled?
    - Are your logistics optimized to minimize carbon emissions?

Examples:
- *Packaging company:* a packaging company might analyze its reliance on single-use plastics and consider transitioning to biodegradable materials.
- *Nonprofit:* a nonprofit running community programs might evaluate its transportation methods, opting for carpooling or electric vehicles for staff and volunteers.
- *Government organization:* a public works department could assess construction practices, transitioning to sustainable materials like recycled asphalt or concrete.

- **Measure your outputs**
  Finally, assess what your organization produces or impacts. This could include carbon emissions, waste output, or community benefits.

  Key questions to ask:
  - What is your carbon footprint, and how can you reduce it?
  - Are you creating unnecessary waste, and can you implement better disposal or recycling systems?
  - What tangible benefits are you delivering to your community or stakeholders?

  Examples:
  - *Tech company:* a tech company might measure the energy efficiency of its data centers and set targets to achieve carbon neutrality.
  - *Nonprofit:* a nonprofit providing educational services might track the number of students served and the measurable improvements in their outcomes.
  - *Government organization:* a transit authority could calculate its public transportation system's emissions and explore options to introduce electric or hybrid buses.

Action Tip

Use this audit to identify:

1. **Quick wins:** small, actionable changes that can create immediate impact, like switching to LED lighting or eliminating unnecessary packaging.
2. **Long-term opportunities:** strategic shifts, like transitioning your entire supply chain to Fair Trade Certified™ vendors or setting a net-zero emissions goal.

By breaking your sustainability audit into these straightforward steps, you'll gain more than just a snapshot of where your business stands – you'll uncover a roadmap for where it can soar. This process will help you discover hidden opportunities to streamline operations, spark innovation, and make a real, measurable impact. With every insight you uncover, you're setting your business up to thrive in ways that resonate with your team, your customers, and the world. Let's turn those "a-ha" moments into action and take your business to the next level.

Step 2: Align Your Supply Chain with Your Purpose

Your supply chain isn't just the plumbing of your business – it's the foundation of your credibility. And just like a leaky pipe, a misaligned supplier can make a mess of your reputation. If your partners' practices contradict your mission, it's like advertising organic apples while your orchard is sprayed with mystery chemicals. Aligning your supply chain with your purpose ensures that every link in the chain supports your mission, so your business talks the talk and walks the walk (preferably in sustainably sourced shoes).

To align your supply chain with your purpose, start by evaluating your current suppliers. Ask yourself: *do their practices align with my purpose? Are they committed to sustainability, ethics, and inclusivity? Do they operate transparently and meet my standards for quality and responsibility?*

For example, a coffee shop dedicated to supporting small farmers might assess its bean suppliers to ensure they're Fair Trade Certified, guaranteeing fair wages and community investment.

Next, create a "supplier code of conduct" – a clear set of guidelines that outline your expectations in key areas like environmental sustainability, ethical practices, and social impact. This document should be non-negotiable, shared with both current and potential suppliers, and supported by regular audits or reports.

Consider Apple's approach: by introducing a supplier code of conduct, they've addressed labor rights, environmental standards, and the integration of recycled materials, setting a high bar for their partners.

Seek out suppliers whose missions align with yours. Certifications and proven track records can be invaluable in identifying partners who share your commitment to ethical and sustainable practices.

For example, Patagonia collaborates exclusively with Fair Trade Certified suppliers, ensuring that every step of their supply chain embodies their mission of environmental stewardship and social equity.

Tracking and monitoring supplier performance is crucial for accountability. Regular audits, performance metrics, and open communication can help ensure compliance with your code of conduct.

A small clothing brand, for instance, might conduct quarterly reviews with suppliers, tracking metrics such as water usage and labor practices to ensure alignment with their sustainability goals.

Finally, foster continuous improvement by collaborating with your suppliers. Share your goals, provide resources or training, and cultivate a shared mission.

A nonprofit focused on food insecurity, for example, might work with local farmers to implement sustainable agricultural methods, creating a supply chain that reflects their mission to reduce waste and enhance community access to healthy food.

Action Tip
Begin by drafting a supplier code of conduct tailored to your purpose and share it with your current suppliers. Evaluate where changes can be made and embrace the mindset that this process is about progress, not perfection. Each step you take toward aligning your supply chain strengthens your commitment to embedding purpose into every aspect of your operations. (Want help? I've got you! A sample supplier code of conduct is available for download in the Net-Positivity Toolkit.)

Step 3: Build Community Impact Programs
Your operations don't exist in a vacuum – they're deeply connected to the communities around you. Instilling purpose means actively considering how your business can create positive knock-on effects in those communities. This isn't about charity; it's about using your unique skills, resources, and expertise to create programs that align with your purpose and make a tangible difference.

Community-impact programs create a sense of shared value. When businesses give back meaningfully, they build stronger ties with the communities they serve, enhance their reputation, and inspire loyalty among employees and customers. These programs amplify your purpose, making it visible and measurable.

Let's take a closer look at some standout examples of businesses that have woven community impact into the fabric of their operations, showing how purpose can drive real-world change.

- **Ben & Jerry's: "Caring Dairy" Program:** Ben & Jerry's supports local farmers through its Caring Dairy initiative, which encourages sustainable farming practices. By providing resources and guidance, they help farmers adopt eco-friendly techniques that benefit the environment while ensuring high-quality ingredients for their

Supplier Code of Conduct Template: for Different Organizations

Below are sample Supplier Codes of Conduct tailored for three types of organizations: a start-up, a mid-size business, and a nonprofit or government organization. Each template emphasizes core values such as sustainability, ethics, and while aligning with the organization's mission and size.

1. Supplier Code of Conduct for a Start-Up

Purpose:

As a start-up, we are committed to building a strong foundation based on integrity, sustainability, and ethical practices. Our suppliers are critical partners in helping us achieve our mission while staying true to our values.

Core Principles:

1. Ethical Business Practices:
   Suppliers must conduct business with honesty and integrity, ensuring compliance with all applicable laws, including anti-corruption and anti-bribery regulations.
2. Sustainability:
   We prioritize suppliers who use renewable resources, minimize waste, and actively reduce their carbon footprint.
   - Example: Recyclable packaging or energy-efficient production methods.
3. Fair Labor Standards:
   Suppliers must ensure fair wages, sate working conditions, and no use of forced or child labor.
4. Transparency:
   Open communication is essential. Suppliers must disclose sourcing practices and provide documentation upon request.

Accountability:

Regular audits and feedback loops will ensure alignment with our values. Non-compliance will lead to review and potential termination of contacts.

Image 1.2: Supplier Code of Conduct from The Net-Positivity Framework Toolkit

products. This program aligns perfectly with their mission of environmental stewardship and social responsibility.
- **TOMS: "One for One" Model:** TOMS built its brand on the promise of giving back. For every pair of shoes sold, the company donates a pair to someone in need. This "One for One" model has provided millions of shoes globally, making TOMS synonymous with purpose-driven impact.
- **REI: Outdoor Stewardship:** REI invests in "outdoor stewardship" programs, partnering with local communities to protect public lands and promote sustainability. They engage customers and employees in their mission, hosting clean-up events and conservation efforts that connect people to their purpose of protecting nature.

So, let's map out the steps of how you can build a community impact program for your business:

1. **Assess your unique strengths:** think about your business's core competencies and resources. What can you offer that will make a meaningful difference?
   - *Tech company example:* offer free coding workshops for underserved youth.
   - *Restaurant example:* partner with local food banks to donate surplus meals.
   - *Government organization example:* host town hall events to improve public access to essential services.
2. **Identify community needs:** engage with local stakeholders to understand what's missing or underserved. Look for areas where your business can bridge the gap.
   - *Example:* a financial services company might notice a lack of financial literacy programs in local schools and offer free workshops.

- *Example:* a retail store might see a need for clothing donations during colder months and organize a community coat drive.

3. **Align programs with your purpose:** your community impact initiatives should reflect your mission. When programs align with your values, they feel authentic and resonate deeply with your audience.
   - If your purpose is sustainability, consider initiatives like tree planting or renewable energy workshops.
   - If your purpose centers on equity, focus on mentoring underrepresented groups or providing scholarships.

4. **Involve your employees:** encourage employees to participate in your community impact programs. This fosters a sense of pride and engagement while amplifying your efforts.
   - Organize volunteer days or matching donation programs.
   - Create internal awards for employees who champion community projects.

5. **Measure and celebrate impact:** track the outcomes of your programs to ensure they're making a difference. Share successes with your team and the community.
   - *Example:* "This year, we donated 10,000 meals, reducing food waste and addressing hunger in our community."
   - Highlight stories of individuals or organizations positively affected by your efforts.

Action Tip

Start small but think big. Identify one immediate way your business can give back to the community and launch a pilot program. For example, a local bookstore could host a monthly literacy event, or a manufacturing company could donate resources to a local trade school.

Community impact programs are about more than giving back – they're about embedding purpose into the DNA of your operations.

By contributing positively to the communities you serve, you strengthen relationships, enhance your brand, and create a legacy of meaningful change. It's not just good business; it's transformative business.

Step 4: Embed Purpose into the Customer Experience

Your purpose shouldn't live quietly behind the scenes – it should shine through every interaction your customers have with your brand. When customers experience your purpose firsthand, they form deeper connections with your business and become loyal advocates for your mission.

Purposeful brands make their mission impossible to miss. Take Warby Parker, for example. Their "Buy a Pair, Give a Pair" program doesn't just talk about social impact – it makes customers a part of it. Every pair of glasses sold means someone in need gets the gift of sight, giving buyers the satisfaction of knowing they're contributing to something bigger than themselves.

Tesla does this, too, by ingraining its purpose into every vehicle it creates. Its mission to "accelerate the world's transition to sustainable energy" isn't just a tagline – it's the very essence of its products. From sleek electric cars to solar-powered charging stations, Tesla turns purpose into a tangible experience customers can see, feel, and drive.

How can you do the same ... or similar?

Think about every touchpoint in your customer journey: marketing, product design, packaging, user experience, and post-purchase follow-ups. These are all opportunities to communicate and amplify your purpose.

- **Marketing that inspires:** Patagonia's ads don't just sell clothes – they tell stories of environmental activism and encourage customers to join the fight to protect the planet.
- **Purposeful packaging:** Allbirds uses recycled materials for its packaging, making sustainability visible from the moment a customer opens the box.

- **Meaningful follow-ups:** after a purchase, TOMS sends updates on the impact made by the customer's contribution, closing the loop and reinforcing their shared purpose.

Action Tip

Audit your customer journey. Map out every interaction customers have with your brand and ask:

- How does this touchpoint reflect our purpose?
- Does it educate, inspire, or connect with customers on a deeper level?
- Are there ways to integrate our mission more authentically?

For example, if you're a local coffee shop with a mission to support sustainable agriculture, you could highlight, on your menu or through social media, the stories of the farmers who grow your beans. If you're a tech company focused on inclusivity, you might ensure your product interfaces are accessible to users of all abilities and share the impact of these choices with your audience.

Lastly, invite your customers to be active participants in your purpose. Whether it's through loyalty programs, community events, or educational campaigns, give them a way to connect with your mission personally. When customers feel like they're part of the journey, your purpose becomes their purpose – and that's where the magic happens.

By embedding purpose into the customer experience, you create not just transactions, but relationships. And those relationships? They're the foundation of a thriving, purpose-driven business.

Step 5: Empower Your Employees – the Heartbeat of Your Business

If your business were a car, your employees wouldn't just be the engine – they'd be the fuel, the GPS, and even the playlist keeping the journey exciting. They're the heartbeat of your operations, and when they're engaged, empowered, and aligned with your purpose, the difference is nothing short of transformative. Happy employees don't just work harder – they work smarter, with passion, creativity, and a drive to see your mission succeed.

Here's the truth: you can't claim to be a purpose-driven business without caring deeply about your team. Your employees are the ones who bring your purpose to life, and empowering them is just as important as setting bold goals or designing a sustainable product.

What does empowerment look like in action?

1. **Giving employees a role in purpose:** Let's take Salesforce's 1-1-1 philanthropy model. By dedicating one percent of equity, one percent of product, and one percent of employee time to charitable initiatives, Salesforce doesn't just promote philanthropy – it makes every employee a contributor to the company's mission. Whether they're volunteering at local schools or developing software for nonprofits, employees feel they're making a difference beyond their job description.

2. **Aligning employee growth with purpose:** Unilever knows that sustainability isn't just about products – it's about people. That's why the company integrates sustainability training into its employee development programs. By teaching team members how their roles connect to the company's mission, Unilever turns employees into ambassadors for its values, ensuring that purpose is embedded into every layer of the organization.

3. **Recognizing purpose-driven excellence:** The best purpose-driven companies celebrate their employees as much as their profits. For example, Patagonia encourages employees to take paid "Environmental Internships" with nonprofit organizations working on issues they're passionate about. This not only boosts morale but also reinforces the company's commitment to environmental stewardship.

Some Ways You Can Empower Your Team

Start with these actionable steps to ensure your employees feel connected to your purpose and valued for their contributions:

1. **Offer purpose-aligned training:** Host workshops or training programs that help employees understand how their roles contribute to your mission. For example, a renewable energy company could train staff on the environmental impact of their projects, giving them the knowledge to champion sustainability both at work and in their communities.
2. **Recognize employees who embody your values:** Create recognition programs that highlight team members who go above and beyond to align their work with your mission. For example, you might offer an "Impact Champion" award to employees who lead community initiatives or implement sustainable practices in their departments.
3. **Provide opportunities to contribute to impact initiatives:** Encourage employees to get hands-on with your purpose. Whether it's through volunteer programs, mentorship opportunities, or cross-departmental projects, give them ways to actively contribute. For instance, a nonprofit focused on food security could invite employees to participate in food drives or urban garden projects.

Why Empowerment Matters

Here's the bottom line: happy, engaged employees create ripple effects that touch every aspect of your business. They provide better customer experiences, bring innovative ideas to the table, and build a culture that attracts top talent. In short, empowered employees are your most valuable asset in driving both profit and purpose.

Action Tip

Start small. Create a "Purpose in Action" day where employees can dedicate time to an impact project of their choice. Or roll out a training session that connects your mission to their daily work. Whatever you do, make it clear that you see, value, and support your team's role in making your purpose a reality.

When you invest in your employees, they invest in your purpose – and together, you create a business that thrives from the inside out.

Tying It All Together

Sustainable purpose-driven operations aren't about perfection – they're about progress. They're about taking deliberate, measurable steps to align your processes, supply chains, and customer experiences with your mission.

As you implement these strategies, you'll start to see how purpose connects to measurable outcomes like customer loyalty, employee retention, and long-term sustainability.

In the next chapter, we'll dig deeper into how to track and measure these outcomes, ensuring you can demonstrate the tangible impact of your efforts.

So, grab your audit forms and purpose filters, and let's start embedding your vision into your operations – because purpose isn't just something you say; it's something you do.

KEY TAKEAWAYS

Purpose becomes real through action

Embed purpose into daily decisions, processes, and systems to demonstrate authenticity and impact.

- Audit for alignment.
- Empower employees.
- Enhance the customer journey.
- Create community impact.

Pillar 3: Data-Driven Measurement

Measuring What Matters

DATA-DRIVEN MEASUREMENT
Use data to track progress, prove impact and drive decisions.

Imagine you're on a road trip with no GPS, no map, and no idea how much gas is in the tank. Sure, you might stumble across some scenic views, but chances are you'll get lost – or worse, stranded. Running a purpose-driven business without data is the same thing. Without clear, measurable insights, you're just guessing at what works, hoping for the best, and leaving your impact – and profit – up to chance.

Welcome to Chapter 6, where we tackle one of the most important (and often overlooked) pillars of the **Net-Positivity Framework: Data-Driven Measurement**.

Let's be real – measuring purpose might not sound as exciting as launching a bold marketing campaign or unveiling a game-changing product. But here's the truth: without data, purpose-driven strategies are just feel-good ideas. With data? They become powerful, actionable, and – most importantly – provable.

In the world of purpose-driven business, numbers tell the story of your impact. Data isn't just a tool for tracking revenue or measuring market share – it's your key to proving that your purpose-driven strategies are more than just words. But here's the catch: it's not enough to measure something. You need to measure what matters. The right data not only validates your efforts but also guides your decisions, builds trust with stakeholders, and sets you up for long-term success.

In this chapter, we'll explore how to measure what truly matters – digging into data that drives both impact and profitability. We'll break down how to set meaningful goals, track progress, and communicate your results effectively. From understanding the power of "key performance indicators" (KPIs) to leveraging tools such as "social return on investment" (SROI) and sustainability accounting, this chapter will give you the practical know-how to analyze your organization's social, environmental, and financial impact.

And because no one wants a lecture on spreadsheets, we'll keep it engaging with real-world examples of businesses that are nailing the measurement game. By the end, you'll be ready to turn your data into compelling stories that inspire your team and stakeholders – setting the stage for the collaborative leadership we'll explore in Chapter 7.

Why Measuring Matters

Imagine two businesses. The first is a boutique coffee shop that prides itself on sourcing sustainably but has no concrete data to back up its claims. Its marketing materials talk vaguely about "doing good," but when a potential corporate partner asks for proof of its impact, the owners fumble with anecdotal evidence. The opportunity to partner – along with potential funding – vanishes.

Now consider another coffee shop. This one has invested in tracking its impact. It can confidently say, "85 percent of our beans are Fair Trade Certified, and we've reduced single-use plastic waste by 60 percent in the last year." This shop not only secures the partnership but also attracts loyal customers and media attention because of its clear, measurable commitment to sustainability.

The difference between these two businesses?

Data.

The first business relies solely on storytelling and hope, while the second uses evidence to substantiate its mission and drive results.

Data is the backbone of credibility.

For business leaders, entrepreneurs, and change-makers, storytelling is powerful – it captures hearts and inspires action. But without data, your story can fall flat. Data is what turns good intentions into compelling, actionable proof. It builds trust with stakeholders, reassures investors, and motivates teams by showing that their work is making a tangible difference.

Take Patagonia and Unilever, for example – two companies we've mentioned before, and with good reason:

- Patagonia doesn't just claim to care about the planet – it measures its carbon footprint across its supply chain, sets ambitious reduction targets, and reports its progress transparently. This data not only validates Patagonia's environmental claims but also builds trust with its customers and inspires loyalty among employees who share its values.

- Unilever tracks the percentage of its product portfolio that aligns with its Sustainable Living Plan, a framework that ties business success to societal and environmental impact. By sharing this data, Unilever demonstrates that purpose-driven strategies can drive both profitability and measurable impact, reinforcing confidence among investors and stakeholders.

The lesson here is clear: data gives your purpose credibility. It's the difference between saying you're making a difference and proving it.

As a business leader, your decisions shape the future of your organization. Whether you're scaling a startup, leading a nonprofit, or managing a corporate team, data is your compass. It helps you:

- **Validate your efforts:** stakeholders – be they customers, investors, or partners – expect more than promises. They want evidence that your strategies deliver results.
- **Adapt and improve:** measuring progress allows you to identify what's working, what's not, and where to pivot.
- **Build trust:** transparent reporting reassures your audience that you're not just talking the talk but walking the walk.
- **Drive profitability:** data doesn't just measure impact – it reveals opportunities for innovation, efficiency, and growth.

Failing to measure what matters can have real consequences. Beyond missed partnerships or diminished trust, it can lead to wasted resources, poor decision-making, and an inability to adapt to market demands. In today's world, where transparency and accountability are increasingly valued, businesses that don't prioritize data risk being left behind.

For example:

- A tech company promoting "sustainable practices" without tracking its energy usage might be called out by consumers or the media, damaging its brand.
- A nonprofit that can't quantify its impact may struggle to secure funding or attract volunteers.
- A retailer ignoring its carbon emissions might face regulatory penalties as governments tighten environmental laws.

In contrast, businesses that embrace data not only protect themselves from these risks but position themselves as leaders in their fields. They attract talent, customers, and investors who value measurable impact and accountability.

Data isn't just about crunching numbers – it's about telling a credible, actionable story that aligns with your purpose and inspires confidence. By integrating measurement into your purpose-driven strategy, you empower your business to achieve more – more impact, more trust, and more success.

In the sections ahead, we'll explore exactly how to set meaningful goals, track progress, and leverage tools to measure what matters most.

Let's get started.

Turn Your Purpose into Measurable, Transformative Action

Step 1: Set Meaningful Goals

Let's face it: without clear goals, even the most ambitious business strategies can feel like aimless wandering. Goals give you focus, direction, and the energy to move forward. They're not just boxes to check – they're your North Star, lighting the way for your team and proving to your stakeholders that your purpose isn't just talk.

Setting goals should feel empowering, not daunting. Think of it as a chance to dream big but with a plan to make those dreams happen. And when you tie those goals to your purpose, you give your entire organization something to rally behind.

Consider Levi Strauss & Co.

In 2020, Levi's set a bold goal to cut greenhouse gas emissions across its supply chain by 40 percent by 2025. This was a data-backed plan that aligned with their purpose of creating sustainable fashion. By setting clear, measurable targets, they motivated their teams, engaged their suppliers, and built trust with environmentally conscious consumers. As of their latest reports, they're on track to meet their ambitious target, proving that purpose-driven goals can drive real, measurable progress.

Goals aren't just about metrics – they're about inspiration.

Here's how to make goal-setting an exciting and transformative step for your business:

1. **Reconnect with your purpose:** Before diving into numbers, revisit your "why." What impact do you want to make? What does success look like for your purpose? Let this guide your goal-setting process.
   – *Example:* if your purpose is to promote clean energy, your goal might be to transition 80 percent of your operations to renewable energy within five years.

2. **Involve your team:** Goal-setting isn't a top-down activity. Involve your employees, partners, and even customers in the process. Their input can bring fresh ideas and deeper buy-in.
   – *Example:* a small restaurant with a mission to reduce food waste could involve its chefs and staff in setting a goal to donate 10,000 meals to local shelters by the end of the year.

3. **Be bold but realistic:** Ambitious goals are inspiring, but they need to feel achievable. Aim high, but ensure your team can see a clear path forward.

- *Example:* instead of declaring that you'll go carbon neutral in one year, set incremental goals, like reducing emissions by 15 percent annually.

To keep your goals actionable and trackable, use the SMART criteria:

- **Specific:** your goal should be clear and unambiguous.
  - *Example:* instead of "reduce waste," aim for "reduce landfill waste by 25 percent in two years."
- **Measurable:** include metrics to track your progress.
  - *Example:* "Plant 5,000 trees in underserved areas by 2025."
- **Achievable:** set goals that stretch your capabilities but remain attainable.
  - *Example:* a small business might aim for "ten percent of products made with recycled materials by next year."
- **Relevant:** align your goals with your broader purpose and mission.
  - *Example:* a nonprofit focused on education might target "50 new scholarships awarded annually."
- **Time-bound:** set a clear deadline to create urgency and accountability.
  - *Example:* "Achieve 80 percent renewable energy use by December 2027."

Action Tip
Kickstart goal-setting today!

Choose one area of your operations – whether it's your supply chain, product design, or community impact – and set a single, SMART goal. Share it with your team, post it in a visible space, and celebrate every milestone you hit along the way.

Goal-setting doesn't just define where you're going – it creates momentum, inspires action, and sets the stage for measurable impact.

Step 2: Identify the Right Key Performance Indicators (KPIs)

If goals are your North Star, key performance indicators (KPIs) are the compass that keeps you on course. They break down your ambitions into measurable milestones, transforming big ideas into tangible results.

Without KPIs, even the best-intentioned goals risk becoming vague aspirations.

With KPIs, you have a roadmap to success.

But here's the catch: not all KPIs are created equal.

Many businesses make the mistake of tracking the wrong metrics – focusing only on past results rather than the actions that actually drive success. To make a meaningful impact, you need leading indicators that help you adjust course in real time, not just lagging indicators that tell you how you did after it's too late to change anything.

Leading vs. Lagging Indicators: Are You Measuring the Right Things?

One of the biggest pitfalls in KPI selection is relying solely on lagging indicators – metrics that measure what already happened rather than those that help you shape future outcomes.

- **Leading indicators:** these focus on controllable actions that predict future success. They help you make real-time decisions to influence the final results.
- **Lagging indicators:** these track past performance, such as total revenue, employee turnover, or total carbon emissions. While they are important for long-term evaluation, they don't help you make proactive adjustments.

High-performing businesses focus on leading indicators because they create the conditions for success before the final results are in.

For example, let's imagine two companies with the same goal: reducing their carbon footprint.

- **Company A:** says, "We want to lower emissions." This is a noble ambition, but without clear KPIs, they don't know where to start, how to measure progress, or when to celebrate wins. A year later, they're unsure if they've made a difference – or how to communicate it to stakeholders.
- **Company B:** sets a leading KPI to "Reduce carbon emissions per product by 20 percent within two years." They track emissions at each stage of production, measure supplier sustainability compliance, and report quarterly updates. When they hit 15 percent, they celebrate – and refine their strategy to achieve the full 20 percent.

The difference?

KPIs turned Company B's goal into a clear, actionable strategy. Stakeholders saw progress, employees felt engaged, and customers gained confidence in the brand.

How to Choose KPIs That Actually Drive Success

The right KPIs are actionable, controllable, and predictive – not just numbers to check off at the end of the year. Here's how to set KPIs that truly matter:

- **Revisit your goals:** each KPI should tie directly to a strategic goal. If your goal is to reduce carbon emissions, a lagging KPI might track total emissions (useful for reporting), but a leading KPI should measure the percentage of renewable energy used in production or supplier compliance with sustainability policies (which directly influence emissions).
- **Focus on what you can control:** a good KPI measures an action your team can take, not just an outcome that depends on external factors.
    - *KPI:* "Increase customer retention by 20 percent." (This depends on customer behavior, which isn't fully within your control.)

- *Better KPI:* "Ensure 90 percent of customers receive a follow-up within 24 hours." (This is an action your team can take to influence retention.)
- **Make them SMART:** your KPIs should be Specific, Measurable, Achievable, Relevant, and Time-bound.
  - *Example:* instead of "Improve employee well-being," set a KPI like "Implement monthly wellness check-ins and track participation rates at 80 percent by Q3."
- **Track and adjust in real time:** set up frequent check-ins to measure progress and adjust as needed. KPIs are not set in stone – if one isn't driving the right results, refine it!

Real-World KPI Examples (By Category)

To bring this to life, let's explore real-world examples of KPIs across environmental, social, and financial impact categories:

Environmental Impact

- **Carbon emissions:** track emissions per product or across the supply chain.
  - *Example:* Allbirds calculates the carbon footprint of every shoe it produces and shares these numbers with customers, ensuring transparency and accountability.
- **Waste reduction:** measure the percentage of waste diverted from landfills.
  - *Example:* IKEA tracks the proportion of recycled or renewable materials in its products as part of its sustainability commitment.
- **Energy efficiency:** monitor the percentage of energy derived from renewable sources.
  - *Example:* a manufacturing company might set a KPI to power 50 percent of its facilities with solar energy by 2025.

Social Impact

- **Diverse hiring:** track the percentage of employees from underrepresented groups.
  - *Example:* Salesforce publicly shares its diversity statistics and sets annual targets for improvement.
- **Community reach:** measure the number of individuals served through your programs.
  - *Example:* a nonprofit might set a KPI to provide job training to 1,000 people annually.
- **Employee well-being:** track engagement, retention, or access to wellness programs.
  - *Example:* Patagonia encourages employees to take paid volunteer time and tracks participation rates.

Financial Impact

- **Revenue from purpose-driven products:** monitor the percentage of sales from sustainable or socially impactful offerings.
  - *Example:* a fashion brand might aim for 40 percent of its collection to be made from recycled materials.
- **Cost savings from sustainability:** measure savings from energy-efficient processes, waste reduction, or ethical sourcing.
  - *Example:* Unilever tracks cost savings from water-efficient production processes in its factories.
- **ROI on community investments:** measure the financial return or brand loyalty gains from CSR efforts.
  - *Example:* TOMS tracks the impact of its "One for One" giving model on customer retention and new customer acquisition.

Bringing KPIs to Life: The Ben & Jerry's Example

Let's bring KPIs to life with a real-world example that demonstrates how numbers can tell a story, drive action, and build trust.

- **Ben & Jerry's goal:** align their supply chain with their social mission.
  - *KPI:* track the percentage of ingredients in their products that are Fair Trade Certified.
  - *Result:* by monitoring this metric and sharing updates in their annual impact report, they demonstrate progress, build trust, and motivate their team to improve.

Contrast that with a company that claims to care about ethical sourcing but doesn't measure or report on it. Without data, the commitment feels empty, and employees and customers are less likely to believe in the mission.

Get Started: Set Your First KPI Today

If you're new to setting KPIs, start simple:

- Choose one goal (e.g., reducing waste, improving employee engagement, increasing supplier sustainability).
- Define one leading KPI that measures an action you can take (e.g., percentage of suppliers that meet ethical standards, number of employees completing training).
- Track it for a quarter and use the insights to refine your approach.

Remember: KPIs aren't just numbers – they're the story of your impact, written in data. They help you measure progress, communicate success, and adjust your strategy when needed.

So, what's your first KPI going to be?

Let's start tracking.

Step 3: Leverage Tools to Track and Analyze Impact

Tracking and analyzing your impact doesn't mean starting from scratch. Plenty of established tools and frameworks are designed to help businesses, nonprofits, and government organizations measure what matters.

These tools make it easier to translate purpose into measurable data and actionable insights.

The best tool for your organization depends on several factors:

- **Your industry:** different industries have tailored tools. For instance, the Sustainability Accounting Standards Board (SASB) is ideal for businesses wanting to disclose sustainability performance to investors, while nonprofits might benefit more from tools like Social Return on Investment (SROI).
- **Your goals:** if your primary goal is reducing carbon emissions, a carbon accounting platform such as GHG Protocol or Carbon Trust is a great fit. If your goal is broader, a tool such as Impact Reporting and Investment Standards (IRIS+) might be more relevant.
- **Your size and resources:** small businesses or startups might prefer straightforward tools such as spreadsheets or free platforms, while larger organizations could invest in more robust software such as ESG Enterprise or Enablon.

Let's look at some of the most effective tools and frameworks available and explore how they can work for you. These aren't just abstract concepts – they're practical resources that can transform how you measure and communicate your impact. Whether you're running a small startup, leading a nonprofit, or managing a growing business, these tools are designed to help you turn purpose into measurable results. Here's how they can make a difference:

1. **Social Return on Investment (SROI)**
    - *What it does:* measures the social value created for every dollar invested.
    - *Example:* a community nonprofit using SROI might find that for every $1 spent on a youth mentorship program, $4 in societal benefits are generated through reduced crime rates and increased education outcomes.

- *Why it matters:* it connects the dots between your investments and the real-world benefits they create, building a compelling case for stakeholders and funders.

2. **Sustainability Accounting Standards Board (SASB)**
    - *What it does:* provides a framework for businesses to disclose their sustainability performance in a way that's comparable and meaningful to investors.
    - *Example:* a retail chain using SASB might measure the energy efficiency of its stores and report reductions in greenhouse gas emissions as a percentage of revenue growth.
    - *Why it matters:* transparency builds trust with investors and customers, positioning your organization as a leader in sustainability.

3. **Carbon Accounting Tools**
    - *What they do:* platforms such as GHG Protocol and Carbon Trust help businesses measure, manage, and reduce their carbon emissions.
    - *Example:* a midsize manufacturing company using GHG Protocol might discover that transportation accounts for 40 percent of its emissions. Armed with this data, it invests in electric delivery vehicles, reducing emissions by 20 percent within a year.
    - *Why it matters:* carbon accounting isn't just about compliance – it's about finding opportunities to cut costs, improve efficiency, and meet stakeholder demands for climate responsibility.

Now that you know a bit about the established frameworks and tools, let's bring them to life with some real-world success stories that show just how powerful the right data can be. We'll revisit a few companies we've talked about quite a bit in this book, so you can see it in action:

Established Tools and Frameworks that Analyze Impact and Where to Find Them

SROI Resources

Social Return on Investment (SROI) isn't a single tool but rather a framework that helps you measure the social, environmental, and economic value your organization creates. It's widely used by nonprofits, businesses, and government organizations to evaluate the broader impact of their initiatives.

Where to Find SROI Resources:

1. SROI Network/Social Value International
   - The SROI Network, now part of Social Value International, is a leading organization that offers training, certifications, and resources for implementing SROI.
   - Their website includes guidelines, case studies, and tools for calculating SROI effectively.
2. SROI Guide
   - The widely recognized SROI Guide is an excellent starting point for understanding and applying the framework. It's available for free download at SROI Network.
3. SROI Software Tools
   - Platforms like Impact Mapper and Clear Impact Scorecard help integrate SROI analysis into broader impact measurement systems.
   - Some accounting tools, such as Microsoft Power BI, can also be customized to track metrics and financial proxies for SROI calculations.
4. Specialized Consultancies
   - Organizations like NEF Consulting and Social Ventures Australia offer consulting services to help organizations apply SROI in a structured and meaningful way.

SASB Resources

The Sustainability Accounting Standards Board (SASB) provides a widely recognized framework for companies to disclose sustainability-related performance in a way that's comparable and meaningful for investors. SASB standards are organized by industry and focus on the sustainability issues most relevant to financial performance.

Image 1.3: Tools/Framework Resources from The Net-Positivity Framework Toolkit

- **Patagonia and Carbon Accounting:** Patagonia isn't just a brand; it's a movement – and carbon accounting is one of its secret weapons. By using tools to measure emissions across its supply chain, Patagonia pinpointed trouble spots such as fabric production. The result? A pivot to lower-impact materials that slashed supply-chain emissions by 30 percent over five years. It didn't just save money; it solidified Patagonia's role as the eco-warrior of outdoor gear. Bonus: their customers get to feel smug about buying a jacket that's saving the planet one stitch at a time.
- **Ben & Jerry's and SROI:** Ben & Jerry's doesn't just scoop ice cream – it scoops purpose. Using social return on investment (SROI) tools, they measured the impact of their "Fair Trade-sourcing" program. Turns out, every dollar spent on Fair Trade premiums delivers better wages, smarter farming practices, and stronger communities in their supplier regions. It's a triple-scoop win: happy farmers, happy customers, and a happier planet. And yes, it makes their Chunky Monkey taste even better.
- **Unilever and SASB:** Unilever isn't just about soap and mayonnaise – it's about leading the way in sustainability. The company uses the SASB framework to show investors how sustainability boosts performance. By tracking metrics such as water usage and waste reduction, they attracted a wave of ESG-focused investors who wanted to back a business that does good while doing well. Turns out, clean water and clean business practices are a great combination.

So how can you find the perfect tool for your business? It's simpler than you think:

- **Start small:** if you're just getting started, don't stress. Grab a free tool such as Google Sheets or check out the B Impact Assessment platform to track your early progress.

- **Zero in on your goals:** what's your big focus? If it's waste reduction, try tools such as Recycling Trackers. For carbon emissions, platforms such as GHG Protocol are game changers.
- **Think big (eventually):** as you grow, consider tools that can handle more complexity. Platforms such as Enablon or Diligent ESG scale with your needs, so you're covered whether you're running a local coffee shop or expanding globally.

By picking the right tools and committing to tracking your progress, you're not just measuring impact – you're creating a roadmap for success.

Step 4: Track Progress Over Time

Imagine you're trying to get in shape (stick with me here). You don't just hop on the scale once, declare victory, and call it a day. You check in regularly – tracking progress, celebrating wins, and tweaking your routine when something isn't working. The same goes for measuring your business's impact. Tracking progress over time is like that trusty fitness tracker – it keeps you accountable, motivated, and ready to pivot when needed.

Simply stated, measurement isn't a one-and-done task; it's the compass guiding your purpose-driven strategies. Regularly tracking your KPIs ensures your goals stay on course, helps you identify patterns or gaps, and gives you the data to adapt when challenges or opportunities arise.

So, what does tracking your progress actually look like? To answer that question, let's explore some real-world examples that show how businesses are using data not just to stay on track, but to thrive:

- **The food retailer's waste-reduction journey:** one grocery chain set a KPI to reduce food waste by 25 percent. During peak holiday seasons, they noticed a dramatic spike in unsold baked goods. Rather than let those loaves of bread turn into crumbs (pun intended), they partnered with local food banks to create a donation program. By tracking progress over several quarters, they not only hit their waste reduction target but also gained positive press for their community contributions.

- **The tech company's diversity hiring initiative:** a midsized tech firm set a goal to increase diversity in its workforce by 15 percent over three years. Early tracking revealed a significant drop-off at the interview stage for underrepresented groups. Using this data, they revamped their recruitment process, partnered with organizations promoting STEM careers for minorities, and offered unconscious bias training to hiring managers. By year two, they were already halfway to their target.
- **Patagonia's carbon emission dashboard:** Patagonia doesn't just track its carbon footprint – they share it with the world. With a dashboard that's as transparent as a freshly cleaned window, they've built trust with their customers while holding themselves accountable for their sustainability goals.

So how can you track progress like a pro? It's easier than you might think.

1. **Make it routine:** set a schedule for tracking KPIs. Whether it's monthly, quarterly, or yearly, consistency is key. Think of it like checking your credit score – regular updates prevent surprises.
2. **Choose the right tools:** depending on your goals, tools such as GHG Protocol (for emissions tracking) or Recyc-Tracker (for waste monitoring) can be lifesavers. And if you're just starting out, even a well-organized spreadsheet can do the trick. The point is to track progress in a way that's accessible and actionable.
3. **Celebrate milestones:** don't wait until you've fully achieved your goals to celebrate. If you're aiming to reduce energy usage by 20 percent and hit five percent in your first year, that's a win! Pop the metaphorical champagne (or the real kind) and use it to keep momentum going.
4. **Adapt when necessary:** data is your feedback loop. If something's not working, don't double down – pivot. For example, if your

eco-friendly packaging isn't cutting waste as expected, reassess your design or sourcing strategy.

5. **Tell a story:** tracking isn't just about numbers – it's about narrative. Share your progress with your team, stakeholders, and customers. Show them how far you've come and what's next on the journey. Use graphs, dashboards, or even quirky infographics to make it engaging.

Tracking your KPIs is like running a marathon. You don't just sprint to the finish line – you pace yourself, track your miles, hydrate (read: review data), and adjust your stride when things feel off. The checkpoints along the way keep you motivated, and by the time you cross the finish line, you've got the receipts (or the data) to prove you crushed it.

So, let's give it a try.

Pick one KPI to track consistently for the next six months. Start small – use a simple spreadsheet or a free tool – and schedule a time to review it regularly with your team. Celebrate small wins, learn from setbacks, and watch how consistent tracking keeps your business running (and thriving) like a well-oiled machine.

Tracking progress isn't just about staying on course – it's about making the journey meaningful and rewarding for everyone involved.

Step 5: Communicate Results Effectively

Tracking data is just the beginning – communicating it is where the magic happens. After all, what good is all that progress if no one knows about it? Whether you're sharing your results with your team, your customers, or your investors, how you tell the story of your impact can inspire trust, loyalty, and even more positive change.

Think of data as a great meal. Sure, you could throw it all on a plate and hope for the best, but presentation is everything. The same goes for sharing your impact. When you communicate your results in a way that's clear, engaging, and meaningful, you're turning numbers into a story that people care about – and want to be part of.

Tips for communicating your impact:

1. **Use visuals**
   - *Why it works:* people process visuals 60,000 times faster than text (science, folks!). Charts, infographics, and dashboards make complex data digestible.
   - *Example:* Allbirds uses a simple, visual "carbon footprint label" on its products, making it easy for customers to see the environmental impact of their shoes at a glance.

2. **Tell stories**
   - *Why it works:* data gets attention, but stories capture hearts. Pair your metrics with real-life anecdotes to make your impact relatable.
   - *Example:* Patagonia's environmental reports don't just share numbers – they tell stories about the people and places their initiatives are helping, from workers in Fair Trade factories to wildlife in restored habitats.

3. **Be transparent**
   - *Why it works:* people value honesty. Sharing both wins and areas for improvement builds trust and credibility.
   - *Example:* Starbucks doesn't shy away from sharing its sustainability challenges in its annual report, such as struggles to reduce water usage in certain regions. This transparency strengthens its reputation as an authentic, purpose-driven brand.

Let's revisit some of the purpose-driven businesses we've mentioned earlier, to see how they're turning numbers into compelling stories that inspire action and build trust.

- **Ben & Jerry's:** their annual "Impact Report" combines quirky branding with serious metrics. It's full of colorful visuals and easy-

to-read stats, all wrapped up in the company's fun, approachable tone. It's like ice cream for your brain!
- **TOMS:** when customers buy a pair of shoes, they receive updates on the communities that benefited from their purchase. This ongoing connection turns buyers into advocates for the brand's mission.
- **Unilever:** in its Sustainable Living Plan, Unilever uses sleek dashboards to highlight key achievements, such as reduced emissions and improved health for millions of consumers, making its impact digestible and shareable.

Now, let's spice things up with some creative and exciting ways to share your results – because data doesn't have to be dull, and your impact deserves to shine!

- **Host an impact day:** celebrate your progress with an event where employees and stakeholders can see the results firsthand. Think open-house-style presentations, interactive dashboards, and even themed snacks (carbon-neutral cupcakes, anyone?).
- **Create a social media campaign:** share your impact metrics in a series of engaging posts, complete with visuals, employee highlights, and customer testimonials. Use hashtags to rally your audience around your mission.
- **Launch a mini docuseries:** showcase stories of your impact in action. A short video series featuring employees, customers, or community partners can bring your data to life and inspire others to join your journey.
- **Make it interactive:** use tools like an online impact calculator, where customers can see how their purchases contribute to your mission.

Pick one upcoming opportunity to share your impact – whether it's a team meeting, a customer newsletter, or a post on social media. Use visuals, pair data with a story, and be authentic about what you've accomplished and what's still ahead.

When you communicate effectively, your impact isn't just a number – it's a movement, and you're inviting everyone to be a part of it.

Measuring what matters isn't just about crunching numbers – it's about bringing your purpose to life in a way that energizes, motivates, and inspires action. It's about showing the world – and yourself – that your business is more than words on a page. It's a force for good, backed by real results that you can celebrate, build on, and proudly share.

By setting bold, meaningful goals, identifying KPIs that truly reflect your mission, and using the right tools to track progress, you're creating a framework that goes beyond validation. You're setting the stage for innovation, trust, and continuous improvement. And when you share your progress with transparency and creativity, you don't just report data – you tell a story that resonates with everyone involved.

This is where the work gets exciting. You've laid the foundation, and now you have the tools to amplify your purpose with measurable, undeniable proof. So, take those first steps, celebrate the small wins, and keep your eyes on the big picture.

As we step into Chapter 7, we'll shift focus from data to the people who make your purpose-driven journey possible. It's time to bring your team and stakeholders into the fold – because while data lights the way, it's people who walk the path, overcome challenges, and turn vision into impact. Let's harness this momentum and create a culture where everyone is inspired to build a business that thrives on purpose, passion, and measurable success.

Buckle up as our journey continues!

KEY TAKEAWAYS

Data is the foundation of purpose

Measuring impact turns lofty ideals into actionable, credible strategies. Without data, purpose-driven claims lack proof and trust.

- Set meaningful goals (SMART).
- Break goals into measurable milestones (KPIs).
- Leverage tools and frameworks to track and analyze impact (SROI, SASB, GHG Protocol).
- Track progress over time.
- Communicate results effectively.

Data-driven measurement transforms purpose into measurable, transformative action – building credibility, trust, and long-term success.

Pillar 4: Collaborative Leadership

Building Teams and Cultures that Drive Impact

COLLABORATIVE LEADERSHIP
Empower teams to work together, fostering a culture of purpose and teamwork that drives meaningful change.

The "Lone Genius" Myth and the Power of We

If history has taught us anything, it's that the idea of the lone genius changing the world is, well ... mostly a myth. Steve Jobs had Wozniak. Oprah built an empire with an entire team behind her. Even Einstein worked with colleagues who helped refine his theories. And this book? It wasn't written in isolation. I had editors who helped shape my ideas, a design team that brought the cover to life, and an incredible network of supporters who pushed me to put my thoughts on paper. The most successful leaders aren't the ones who try to do it all alone – they're the ones who bring people together, inspire collaboration, and build something greater than the sum of its parts.

In business, the same rule applies. The best ideas, the biggest innovations, and the most lasting impacts don't come from a single executive at the top – they come from teams empowered to think, contribute, and lead together. That's what collaborative leadership is all about. It's not about control; it's about connection. And in this chapter, we'll explore how to build a culture where leadership is a shared mindset that fuels purpose, impact, and long-term success.

What's the secret ingredient to a thriving, purpose-driven business?

Spoiler alert: it's not a groundbreaking product or a revolutionary marketing strategy.

It's people – your team, your partners, your community.

Collaborative leadership is the glue that binds your purpose to real-world impact, turning lofty ideals into actionable results. And here's the kicker: the most innovative ideas, game-changing decisions, and lasting successes rarely come from a single leader. They come from a team empowered to lead together.

Welcome to the fourth pillar of the **Net-Positivity Framework: Collaborative Leadership.**

By now, we've covered purpose-driven vision, operations, and metrics. But get this – none of those pillars stand tall without the right people to build, sustain, and grow them. Leadership isn't about barking orders or sitting at the top of the org chart; it's about creating a culture where everyone feels invested in the mission and equipped to contribute their best.

Think of your business like an orchestra. You're the conductor, ensuring harmony and balance, but every single musician has a critical role to play. When you empower your team to take ownership of their parts, the result isn't just music – it's a symphony. Collaborative leadership is about fostering that sense of ownership, shared purpose, and creativity.

When leaders shift from simply directing to truly engaging their teams, something powerful happens – work becomes more than just tasks and goals; it becomes a shared mission. This shift is at the heart of modern leadership, where success is no longer about authority but about alignment, trust, and co-creation.

Leadership has evolved. That old-school, top-down, command-and-control approach no longer works in today's fast-paced, purpose-driven world. Employees want more than a paycheck – they want to feel part of something bigger. They want leaders who inspire, support, and listen. Collaborative leadership meets these needs by shifting the focus from power to partnership.

Consider this: a Gallup study found that highly engaged teams show 21 percent greater profitability. And yet, only 31 percent of employees in the United States are engaged at work, marking a ten-year low.[7] This decline in engagement underscores the importance of fostering a workplace environment that promotes employee involvement and enthusiasm. Implementing strategies to enhance engagement can lead to significant improvements in productivity and profitability. Collaborative leadership bridges this gap by fostering environments where people feel valued, heard, and empowered to contribute.

Take Microsoft under Satya Nadella's leadership as an example. When Nadella took over as CEO in 2014, he inherited a company that was highly competitive internally, with teams working in silos, and a culture

---

7 Harter, Jim. "U.S. Employee Engagement Sinks to 10-Year Low." *Gallup*, 14 Jan. 2025, https://www.gallup.com/workplace/654911/employee-engagement-sinks-year-low.aspx.

that often rewarded individual success over collective progress. He knew that for Microsoft to remain relevant and innovative, this had to change. Nadella introduced a growth mindset across the organization, encouraging teams to learn from failures, embrace collaboration, and break down barriers between departments.

The impact was transformative. Under his leadership, Microsoft shifted from a "know-it-all" culture to a "learn-it-all" culture, fostering an environment where employees felt empowered to share ideas and experiment without fear of failure. One engineer at Microsoft described the shift as "night and day," saying, "Before, it felt like every team was protecting its turf. Now, we're encouraged to build together and leverage each other's strengths. It's made all the difference in how we innovate."

One of the most significant examples of this cultural shift was the development of "Microsoft Teams."

Before Nadella's leadership, a project like Teams might have been bogged down by internal competition, with separate product teams hesitant to collaborate. Instead, engineers, designers, and product managers from across the company worked together to develop and launch Teams in record time, positioning it as a top competitor to Slack and Zoom. This cross-functional collaboration helped Microsoft capitalize on remote work trends, making Teams a core part of its business strategy.

Nadella's leadership also emphasized empathy and inclusion. In one of his most notable early leadership meetings, he asked executives to share a personal story about an experience that shaped them, reinforcing that vulnerability and connection are critical to strong leadership. Employees responded to this shift with renewed engagement. As one longtime Microsoft employee put it, "It's no longer about who's the smartest in the room; it's about who's willing to listen, learn, and build something better together."

The result? Microsoft is not only a financial powerhouse but also a case study in how inclusive leadership drives innovation and purpose. By shifting the company's focus from internal competition to collaboration, Nadella helped transform Microsoft into one of the most admired and forward-thinking companies in the world.

Ready to unlock the full potential of your team?

Let's look at some strategies that will inspire, empower, and bring out the collaborative genius in everyone.

Lead with Vision, Not Just Direction

Collaborative leaders don't micromanage – they set a clear vision and empower their teams to find the best path forward. Your role is to inspire and align, not dictate.

- *Example:* at Patagonia, the leadership team communicates a crystal-clear purpose – environmental stewardship. Employees are given the autonomy to design programs, develop products, and engage in activism that aligns with this mission.
- *Action tip:* regularly share your organization's purpose with your team. Create opportunities for open dialogue about how their roles contribute to the bigger picture.

Create Psychological Safety

People do their best work when they feel safe to speak up, share ideas, and take risks without fear of ridicule or punishment.

- *Example:* Google conducted a study to understand what makes teams effective. The number one factor? Psychological safety. Teams that felt safe to be vulnerable and take risks outperformed those that didn't.
- *Action tip:* encourage questions, celebrate diverse perspectives, and model vulnerability. Acknowledge your own mistakes to show it's okay to learn and grow.

Align Personal Goals with Organizational Impact

Collaborative leadership means understanding what motivates your team on an individual level and connecting that to your mission.

- *Example:* Salesforce empowers employees through its 1-1-1 model, allowing them to dedicate one percent of their time to philanthropic projects. This not only builds employee engagement but also amplifies Salesforce's broader impact.
- *Action tip:* during check-ins, ask employees what drives them personally and explore how their goals can align with the organization's mission.

Now that we've explored how to inspire teams and foster collaboration, let's dive into the next layer of impactful leadership: building a workplace culture where inclusivity and innovation thrive side by side.

Inclusivity and innovation go hand in hand. Diverse teams bring a wealth of perspectives, leading to better problem-solving and more creative solutions. But building an inclusive culture requires more than hiring diverse talent – it demands a commitment to equity and belonging.

Strategies for Building Inclusion

- **Evaluate representation:** Track diversity metrics and identify gaps in leadership roles, team composition, and recruitment pipelines.
    - *Example:* Unilever implemented inclusive hiring practices and achieved a 50/50 gender balance in management roles by 2020.
- **Invest in equity training:** Offer workshops on unconscious bias, allyship, and inclusive leadership to ensure everyone feels valued.
    - *Example:* Airbnb developed an internal "Belonging Team" focused on creating an inclusive culture, leading to stronger team engagement.
- **Foster belonging:** Celebrate diverse voices and experiences through employee resource groups, storytelling initiatives, or cultural events.

- *Example:* Coca-Cola hosts global heritage celebrations, reinforcing its commitment to inclusion and cultural understanding.

Sparking Innovation Through Collaboration

- **Break down silos:** Encourage cross-departmental collaboration to spark fresh ideas.
  - *Example:* at Pixar, leaders ensure that teams from different disciplines – animators, writers, and developers – collaborate from the start of every project, resulting in groundbreaking films.
- **Reward creativity:** Recognize and reward innovative thinking, even when ideas don't pan out.
  - *Example:* 3M created the "Post-It Note" thanks to a culture that encouraged employees to experiment and share ideas, regardless of hierarchy.

Leadership Strategies for Driving Change

- **Be transparent:** change is hard, but transparency builds trust. Share the "why" behind decisions and involve your team in the process.
- **Champion collaboration at the top:** collaborative leadership starts with you. Lead by example – work across teams, seek input, and show that no idea is too small to consider.
- **Recognize and celebrate impact:** recognize team efforts and highlight how their contributions support your purpose.

Leadership isn't just a role – it's a mindset.

As we've explored in this chapter, the success of your net-positive initiatives hinges on the way you lead, inspire, and empower the people around you. Collaborative leadership is the driving force behind a purpose-driven organization. It's about creating a culture where your team feels valued, your partners feel engaged, and everyone is aligned around a shared mission to make an impact.

Let's revisit the key strategies we've covered in this chapter:

1. **Inspiring teams and fostering collaboration:** Leadership isn't about being the loudest voice in the room – it's about listening, elevating diverse perspectives, and encouraging open dialogue. By building trust and a sense of ownership, you enable your team to transform ideas into action.
2. **Building an inclusive and innovative workplace culture:** Inclusivity isn't just a moral imperative; it's a business advantage. Innovation thrives when every team member feels safe to bring their authentic self to work. From diversifying hiring practices to promoting psychological safety, inclusion is the foundation of sustainable success.

These strategies aren't just theoretical – they're the blueprint for building an organization where purpose is not just a statement, but a way of life. Your leadership style directly shapes how effectively your business delivers on its net-positive initiatives. It determines whether your team feels empowered to innovate, whether your culture attracts the right talent, and whether your mission resonates with the people who matter most: your employees, customers, and community.

As we close this chapter, it's time to take everything we've learned about leadership and culture and put it into practice. This book isn't just about understanding net-positive principles – it's about applying them in ways that transform your business.

In the next part of this journey, Part III: The What –Taking Action, we'll move from the "why" and the "how" to the "what."

It's time to roll up your sleeves and dive into the tools that will help you operationalize purpose within your organization.

Chapter 8 will equip you with actionable resources, including sustainability audits, KPI trackers, and DEI roadmaps. These tools will bridge the gap between strategy and execution, giving you the practical means to assess, measure, and refine your impact.

The path forward is exciting, challenging, and deeply rewarding. Leadership is the catalyst that makes all this possible – but tools are the gears that keep the engine running. Together, they create a business that doesn't just survive – it thrives by making a measurable difference in the world.

So, take a deep breath, reflect on what kind of leader you want to be, and get ready to build something extraordinary. The journey from purpose to action is where transformation begins.

Let's dive in.

KEY TAKEAWAYS

Leadership is about empowering people

Collaborative leadership shifts focus from authority to partnership, creating a culture where everyone feels invested in the mission and equipped to contribute.

- Lead with vision and trust.
- Foster psychological safety.
- Align personal and organizational goals.
- Champion inclusivity and innovation.
- Model and celebrate collaboration.

Collaborative leadership is the key to activating purpose and driving sustainable impact, creating an environment where teams, partners, and communities thrive together.

PART III
THE WHAT

Taking Action

With a strong foundation in place, it's time to bring your purpose-driven strategy to life. Part III: The What – Taking Action provides the tools, case studies, and industry-specific insights to help you implement and sustain net-positive practices. From sustainability audits and KPI trackers to long-term planning and leadership strategies, Chapters 8–13 will guide you in making a measurable impact and leaving a lasting legacy.

8

Tools for Transformation

Sustainability Audits, KPI Trackers, and DEI Roadmaps

Imagine trying to assemble IKEA furniture without the instruction manual. You might get the job done … eventually. But it'll take twice as long, there will be a few screws left over, a few choice words might be said, and there's a good chance your new bookshelf is going to collapse at the slightest breeze. Running a purpose-driven business without the right tools is kind of like that – you might have a vision, but without a clear framework, things get messy, slow, and frustrating.

That's why this chapter isn't just about ideas; it's about execution. Whether you're tracking sustainability efforts, measuring impact with KPIs, or building a truly inclusive workplace with a DEI roadmap, having the right tools in place ensures your mission is measurable, scalable, and successful. The difference between businesses that thrive with purpose and those that struggle isn't passion – it's process. And that's exactly what we're about to build.

Before starting this chapter, you did the foundational work to define your purpose, align your operations, measure your impact, and cultivate a culture of collaboration.

It's time to shift gears and move from planning to execution.

Welcome to Part III: The What – Taking Action. This is where strategy meets momentum, where big ideas take shape, and where your business's purpose comes to life in measurable, actionable ways.

In this chapter, we'll learn a bit more about the practical resources and frameworks that empower you to act with clarity and confidence. Think of this chapter as your blueprint – equipped with the tools you need to ensure your efforts are not just impactful but also measurable and scalable; these tools will help you take purposeful strides toward lasting transformation.

This is the turning point where your commitment to purpose evolves into real-world results. This chapter equips you with the resources you need to make purpose-driven business a daily reality.

Picture this: you've just opened a 1,000-piece puzzle box. You're excited and you can't wait to see it come together. But then you realize: there's no picture to guide you. No frame to start with. Just a sea of scattered pieces and a vague sense of what it *should* look like. That's exactly what it feels like to run a purpose-driven business without the right tools. You might have the passion and the big-picture vision, but without a clear framework, strategy becomes guesswork, and momentum gets lost in the mess.

I've seen it firsthand. Early in my career, I worked with organizations bursting with purpose – powerful missions, passionate teams, and the drive to make a difference. But without systems in place to guide their execution, progress was slow and hard to measure. Great ideas stalled. Teams got frustrated. Funders asked for impact data that didn't exist.

Then we brought in tools – sustainability audits, KPI trackers, DEI roadmaps –and everything changed. Suddenly, those same organizations had clarity. They could prioritize the right actions, measure what mattered, and celebrate wins along the way. Their purpose stopped living only in slide decks and mission statements – it showed up in their daily work, their decision-making, and their results.

That's the power of the right tools. A sustainability audit doesn't just assess your footprint – it reveals where to reduce waste, save money, and build credibility with conscious consumers. KPI trackers don't just record numbers – they shine a light on what's working (and what's not), helping you make smarter decisions, faster. And a DEI roadmap? It's the difference between performative statements and transformative change – guiding your team through tangible actions that create more inclusive, equitable workplaces.

These aren't just checklists – they're your puzzle's edge pieces. They help frame your vision, give your team direction, and ensure every action aligns with your purpose.

Because here's the truth: **without tools, purpose-driven business is an aspiration. With tools, it becomes a strategy**.

Let's dive in and explore how these tools can help your purpose come to life –measurably, consistently, and with impact that truly lasts.

Tool 1: Sustainability Audits

A sustainability audit is the ultimate health checkup for your business's environmental impact. It's about more than identifying what you're doing wrong – it's about celebrating what you're doing right and discovering opportunities for meaningful improvement. From the energy you consume to the waste you produce, a sustainability audit evaluates your inputs (what you bring in), processes (how you operate), and outputs (what you produce or impact).

Understanding your environmental footprint is the first step toward reducing it. A sustainability audit helps you pinpoint inefficiencies, lower costs, and align with customer and stakeholder expectations.

A sustainability audit might sound complex, but it's a practical and impactful process that can transform your business operations.

Here's how to conduct one, step-by-step, with real-world examples and tools to guide you.

1. **Define your scope**

   Before you dive in, decide what parts of your business to evaluate. Will you focus on energy use, waste management, sourcing practices, emissions, or all the above? Defining your scope ensures you stay focused and actionable.
   - *Example:* a small café might start with waste management, looking at how much food and packaging waste they generate. A manufacturing company might prioritize emissions and water usage.
   - *Pro tip:* start small. Choose one or two areas where you think you can make the biggest impact or where you're spending the most money.

2. **Gather data**

   This is where the detective work begins. Collect information about your operations that corresponds to your scope. Look at energy bills, waste logs, transportation records, and supplier certifications.
   - *Example:* a retail clothing brand might pull data from their warehouses on packaging waste and energy consumption.
   - *Fun fact:* data can sometimes surprise you! One bakery discovered its ovens were using 40 percent more energy than necessary due to outdated equipment.

3. **Assess your impact**

   Once you have your data, analyze it to understand your environmental footprint.
   - *Example:* a tech company might discover that employee commuting and data-center energy-use account for most of its carbon footprint.
   - *Pro tip:* if you're feeling overwhelmed, there are consultants and platforms (such as Sustainable Business Consulting or GreenStep Solutions) that can help interpret your data.
   - *Well-recognized audit framework:* many companies use the GHG Protocol for carbon accounting – it's the gold standard for emissions measurement.

4. **Identify opportunities**

   This is the exciting part – spotting areas for improvement. Divide your findings into "quick wins" (things you can tackle right away) and "long-term strategies" (bigger projects that require more planning).
   - *Quick win example:* a local brewery swapped out traditional light bulbs for LEDs, cutting energy costs by 20 percent in a month.
   - *Long-term example:* an apparel company, like Patagonia, revamped its entire supply chain, switching to recycled fabrics and reducing emissions by 30 percent over five years.
   - *Tip for small businesses:* don't underestimate the power of small changes. Even reducing packaging by ten percent can make a big impact over time.

5. **Create an action plan**

   Outline the specific steps you'll take to address inefficiencies, assign responsibilities to team members, and set realistic timelines. This is your roadmap for turning insights into action.

- *Example:* a hotel chain might assign its sustainability officer to implement a water-saving initiative, replacing old fixtures with low-flow alternatives within 12 months.
- *Real-life case:* IKEA used its sustainability audit to set a bold goal: 100 percent renewable energy use by 2030. Their action plan included installing solar panels at stores and improving energy efficiency across operations.

Your sustainability audit isn't just a one-off project – it's a tool for transformation. By systematically analyzing your operations, you uncover opportunities to save money, reduce waste, and strengthen your reputation as a purpose-driven business.

It's now your turn: where will your sustainability audit take you?

Tool 2: KPI Trackers

KPI trackers are like the heartbeat monitors of your business, keeping you informed about the metrics that matter most to your purpose-driven goals. Whether it's tracking carbon reductions, diversity hiring rates, or the measurable impact of your community programs, these trackers turn big, lofty aspirations into tangible, actionable data points.

Here's why they're essential: KPIs take the guesswork out of progress. They transform abstract goals into concrete numbers, giving you a clear view of what's working, what's not, and where you might need to pivot. Without them, you're flying blind – relying on anecdotes or gut feelings instead of facts. With KPIs in place, every decision you make is rooted in data, ensuring you stay aligned with your mission and can confidently showcase your progress to stakeholders.

Let's break down how to implement KPI tracking into your business operations. It's simpler than you think, and the payoff is immense.

Here's how you can get started:

1. **Identify your KPIs**

   Use the SMART criteria to ensure your KPIs are Specific, Measurable, Achievable, Relevant, and Time-bound.
   - *Environmental:* carbon emissions per product or percentage of renewable energy used.
   - *Social:* percentage of diverse hires or number of community partnerships.
   - *Financial:* revenue from sustainable products or cost savings from energy efficiency.

2. **Choose your tracking tool**

   Start with simple options such as Google Sheets, or explore platforms such as B Impact Assessment for more robust tracking.

3. **Set benchmarks**

   Determine your baseline and set realistic targets for improvement.

4. **Monitor progress**

   Schedule regular check-ins – weekly, monthly, or quarterly – to review data and assess progress.

5. **Adjust as needed**

   Use your insights to refine strategies and address challenges.

Example in Action

Allbirds Tracks Carbon Footprints and Builds Customer Loyalty.

Allbirds, the eco-friendly footwear and apparel company, has built its brand on sustainability and transparency. Central to their strategy is their commitment to tracking and sharing the carbon footprint of every product they make. This isn't just a one-off marketing ploy – it's a deeply ingrained practice that drives both accountability and trust.

For example, Allbirds calculates the carbon emissions of its materials, manufacturing processes, and transportation for every shoe. They report this data on their website and even print the carbon footprint of each product directly on the item's label. A standard pair of Allbirds shoes, for instance, might have a carbon footprint of 7.6 kilograms of CO_2e (carbon dioxide equivalent), compared to the average sneaker, which typically emits about 12.5 kilograms of CO_2e.

But Allbirds don't stop at measurement. They've committed to reducing these numbers. By switching to materials such as sugarcane-derived SweetFoam for their soles and responsibly sourced merino wool, they've slashed emissions in key areas of their supply chain. They've also invested in renewable energy projects and offset their remaining emissions to achieve net-zero carbon neutrality.

The results are compelling. According to the company's sustainability reports, these efforts have reduced their carbon intensity per product by nearly ten percent over three years. Beyond the environmental impact, this transparency has resonated with customers.

A 2018 Nielsen study revealed that 73 percent of global consumers are willing to change their shopping habits to reduce environmental impact[8] and a 2023 article by McKinsey & Company, in collaboration with NielsenIQ, highlighted that 78 percent of U.S. consumers consider a sustainable lifestyle important.[9] Allbirds' approach speaks directly to this demand, fostering loyalty among eco-conscious buyers who see their purchases as a vote for sustainable practices.

Allbirds' carbon tracking isn't just a tool for internal improvement – it's a cornerstone of their brand identity. By putting numbers to their purpose and sharing them openly, they've cultivated a reputation as a company that doesn't just talk about sustainability but lives it. This approach not only attracts customers but also inspires other businesses to follow their lead, amplifying their impact beyond their own operations.

---

8   Nielsen, *What Sustainability Means to Consumers Today*, Nielsen, 11 Oct. 2018, https://www.nielsen.com/insights/2018/what-sustainability-means-today/.
9   NielsenIQ and McKinsey & Company, "Consumers Care About Sustainability – and Back It Up with Their Wallets," *NielsenIQ*, 6 Feb. 2023, https://nielseniq.com/global/en/insights/report/2023/consumers-care-about-sustainability-and-back-it-up-with-their-wallets/.

Here's something I want to emphasize – you don't need to start at Allbirds' level. You don't have to calculate every nuance of your carbon footprint on day one or launch a full-scale reporting system tomorrow. The key is to start *somewhere*.

Maybe it's tracking one metric that matters to your business, such as energy use or waste reduction. Or perhaps it's setting a small, tangible goal, such as sourcing ten percent of your materials from sustainable suppliers. The point is to get started.

Data isn't just for global brands or massive operations – it's for anyone committed to making an impact. Begin today, and like Allbirds, you'll find that small steps can lead to big results.

Tool 3: DEI Roadmaps – Building Cultures that Reflect Purpose

A DEI (Diversity, Equity, and Inclusion) roadmap is your company's strategic plan to foster a workplace culture that celebrates diverse perspectives and provides equitable opportunities for all. It's not just about checking a box; it's about embedding inclusivity into every facet of your operations, ensuring your team mirrors the rich diversity of the communities you work with and serve.

Organizations with inclusive cultures outperform their peers. Studies by McKinsey & Company show that companies in the top quartile for ethnic and gender diversity are 35 percent more likely to outperform their competitors financially.[10] Beyond numbers, inclusive workplaces foster innovation, engagement, and trust, creating an environment where everyone can contribute their best. A DEI roadmap ensures that these values move from ideals to actionable strategies.

---

10 Vivian Hunt et al., "Why Diversity Matters," *McKinsey & Company*, 1 Jan. 2015, https://www.mckinsey.com/capabilities/people-and-organizational-performance/our-insights/why-diversity-matters.

Here are your step-by-step instructions for building your DEI Roadmap:

1. **Assess your current state**

   The first step to building a DEI roadmap is understanding where your organization currently stands. Use tools such as employee surveys, anonymous feedback, or focus groups to gauge perceptions around inclusivity, equity, and representation.

   - *Real-world example:* after a diversity audit revealed significant gaps in representation and inclusivity, Netflix launched a comprehensive initiative to transform its workplace culture. This included creating the "Inclusion Strategy Team" to focus on hiring, retaining, and promoting underrepresented talent across all levels. The company also introduced public-facing transparency reports to track progress, signaling a long-term commitment to accountability and inclusivity. This effort not only enhanced internal engagement but also positioned Netflix as a leader in fostering diversity within the entertainment industry.
   - *Action tip:* don't be afraid to uncover hard truths. Growth begins with an honest baseline.

2. **Define goals**

   Clear, measurable goals are the foundation of any successful DEI strategy. Align these goals with your overall mission and priorities.

   - *Examples:*
     - Increasing the percentage of underrepresented groups in leadership roles by 20 percent within three years.
     - Launching mentorship programs to support career advancement for employees from diverse backgrounds.
     - Building supplier diversity programs that prioritize partnerships with minority-owned businesses.

In my experience, goals rooted in authenticity resonate most. At an organization I worked with, introducing a mentorship program for underrepresented staff transformed morale and retention – proof that a little investment in people yields enormous returns.

3. **Develop initiatives**

   Once goals are set, identify the specific actions to achieve them.
   - *Examples:*
     - Offering bias training for hiring managers to create equitable hiring practices.
     - Partnering with local organizations to diversify talent pipelines.
     - Reviewing pay equity and addressing disparities.
   - *Real-world example:* Unilever's leadership program incorporates DEI principles by requiring managers to mentor employees from diverse backgrounds. This initiative led to a 50 percent increase in women in management roles globally.
   - *Action tip:* don't overcomplicate. Focus on initiatives that align with your organization's capacity and strengths.

4. **Track progress**

   Metrics are your roadmap's compass. Regularly track key performance indicators (KPIs) such as representation at different levels, employee satisfaction scores, retention rates, and participation in DEI initiatives.
   - *Real-world example:* Google publishes an annual diversity report that outlines representation data, hiring trends, and areas for improvement. This transparency builds trust with employees and stakeholders.
   - *Pro tip:* transparency around challenges and progress reinforces commitment. Celebrate wins but acknowledge areas needing growth.

5. **Communicate results**

    Share updates with your team, customers, and stakeholders to demonstrate accountability. Use visuals such as infographics or dashboards to make data engaging and accessible.

    – *Real-world example:* Salesforce shares its DEI progress through its Equality Report, which highlights data on representation, initiatives, and stories from employees. By combining metrics with personal narratives, they humanize the data, building a stronger connection with their audience.

In a previous leadership role I held, I found sharing small wins – such as an increase in diverse hires or successful employee-led DEI events – energized our team and inspired further buy-in.

When used consistently, DEI roadmaps help organizations:

- Build cultures of trust and transparency.
- Create equitable opportunities that unlock innovation.
- Align internal practices with external impact, ensuring your purpose isn't just words – it's action.

In Chapter 9, you'll see how businesses have successfully implemented sustainability audits, KPI trackers, and DEI roadmaps to transform their operations and amplify their impact. You don't need to have it all figured out to begin. Start where you are, take the first step, and let these tools guide you toward the purpose-driven success your organization can achieve.

Let's turn your vision into a workplace culture that thrives – because when everyone has a seat at the table, we all rise.

KEY TAKEAWAYS

Purpose needs actionable tools

Sustainability audits, KPI trackers, and DEI roadmaps are essential resources to turn your purpose-driven goals into measurable, scalable, and impactful outcomes.

- Sustainability audits drive efficiency and impact.
- KPI trackers provide clear progress.
- DEI roadmaps build inclusive cultures.
- Data makes purpose tangible.

These tools empower businesses to operationalize purpose, track progress, and create lasting transformation in both impact and profitability.

9

Real-World Success Stories
Lessons From Net-Positive Leaders

Let me share a funny story I was once told. I don't know if this story is real or not – but this is how it goes.

Years ago, a well-meaning CEO of a midsized company decided to launch a sustainability initiative with a bold first step – cutting the company's energy usage by half. The problem? He forgot to tell anyone! One Monday morning, employees walked into an office that looked like the set of a horror film: lights dimmed to a flicker, printers unplugged, and the coffee machine completely lifeless (imagine the horror!). The IT department scrambled to reboot servers. Accountants worked by the glow of their phone screens. And one particularly resourceful employee conducted a budget meeting using a flashlight.

The lesson? Good intentions don't translate into real impact unless they're backed by strategy, communication, and a solid plan.

That's what this chapter is all about – real-world stories of companies that got it right. Whether it's sustainability, DEI, or transparency, these businesses turned purpose into action, and their lessons are packed with insights (and hopefully fewer power outages) for your own journey.

Welcome to Chapter 9, where we leave the theoretical behind and dive into real-world *success* stories. These are businesses and organizations that didn't just talk about going net-positive; they made it happen. And here's the best part: they're not all billion-dollar giants. Whether you're a startup, a nonprofit, or a midsize business, these stories will show you that transformation is possible – no matter where you're starting.

I know this because I've been there myself. I've worked with organizations that, at first glance, felt miles away from achieving their goals. I've seen teams overwhelmed by the sheer weight of where they wanted to go, and I've watched as they took those first courageous steps.

One of the most rewarding moments in my career came from guiding a small nonprofit to rethink their operations and align them with a bigger purpose. They started with just a sustainability audit and a few modest goals – such as reducing paper waste and creating partnerships with local eco-friendly vendors. Today, they're an example of what purpose-driven transformation looks like at a grassroots level, inspiring their community and attracting new donors.

Another experience that's stuck with me involved a midsize business trying to integrate diversity, equity, and inclusion into their hiring practices. At first, it was daunting; change always is. But by taking small, measurable steps – such as revising job descriptions and creating mentorship opportunities – they saw not only an increase in diverse talent but also a noticeable shift in workplace culture. And the best part? That ripple effect extended far beyond their office walls.

What these experiences have taught me – and what you'll see in the stories ahead – is that progress isn't reserved for the giants of the world.

It's achievable for anyone who's willing to start, adapt, and commit to aligning their operations with their values.

By the end of this chapter, you'll not only feel inspired but armed with actionable insights to apply to your own journey. Plus, we'll sprinkle in some lessons from my personal experiences (and occasional missteps) for good measure.

Let's dig in!

Case Study 1: IKEA – Sustainability, Simplified

IKEA recognized that its massive global footprint came with significant environmental responsibilities. Producing billions of products annually while addressing environmental impact wasn't just a logistical challenge – it was a moral imperative. They needed a plan that would meet the needs of their business while addressing the increasing expectations of environmentally conscious consumers.

The Net-Positive Move IKEA Made

In 2012, IKEA made the ambitious commitment to using 100 percent renewable or recycled materials in all its products by 2030. To achieve this, they also invested heavily in energy efficiency, transitioning stores to solar power, and purchasing wind farms to offset their energy use. Additionally, IKEA took steps to empower its customers to live more sustainably, offering tips on furniture care, upcycling, and recycling.

With their bold commitments in place, IKEA rolled up their sleeves and set out to turn their net-positive vision into measurable action.

Here's how their journey has unfolded so far.

- By 2022, over 70 percent of IKEA's product range incorporated renewable or recycled materials.

- The company became one of the world's largest private producers of renewable energy, generating more than two-thirds of the energy used across its operations.
- IKEA launched initiatives such as the "Buy Back" program, encouraging customers to return old furniture for resale or recycling, reducing waste and extending the life of its products.

Of course, no transformation comes without its share of challenges. Along the way, IKEA encountered hurdles that offered valuable lessons and opportunities for growth. Early in their sustainability efforts, they faced criticism for the labor practices of some of their suppliers. This exposed the need for rigorous audits and better supply-chain transparency. They also underestimated the scale of the challenge in sourcing recycled materials at scale, which delayed some product rollouts. These missteps reinforced a critical lesson: sustainability isn't a straight path – it requires continuous adaptation, transparency, and the willingness to learn from setbacks.

Through their journey, IKEA discovered key insights that not only shaped their strategy but also offer practical guidance for any organization striving to go net-positive.

A few of those lessons learned include:

- **Set ambitious but achievable goals:** IKEA's 2030 target is a long-term vision that recognizes the importance of steady, measurable progress. By breaking the journey into manageable steps, they've maintained momentum while avoiding burnout.
- **Engage your supply chain:** sustainability doesn't stop at your front door. IKEA's collaboration with suppliers to source recycled and renewable materials ensures alignment across the entire production process.
- **Think beyond the product:** IKEA's efforts extend past the furniture they sell, educating customers on sustainable living and offering solutions for furniture disposal, repair, and recycling.

These takeaways aren't just for IKEA – they're stepping stones for any business looking to start its own net-positive journey. You don't need to be a global giant to take meaningful steps toward sustainability. Maybe you're not ready to build wind farms or launch large-scale buy-back programs, but you can start small.

Could you switch your office lighting to LED bulbs? Source recycled materials for your products? Offer customers a recycling program for packaging or products? Each step – no matter how small – contributes to a bigger transformation.

IKEA's story reminds us that sustainability is a long-term commitment that evolves over time. By setting bold goals, engaging your team and partners, and staying open to feedback and adjustments, you can build a more sustainable future – one step at a time.

Case Study 2: Patagonia – Putting Purpose First

Patagonia has built a reputation as a brand that prioritizes the planet over profits. However, they knew that vocal advocacy alone wasn't enough – they wanted their business model to serve as a shining example of sustainability in action. The challenge was immense: how could they continue to grow their brand while staying true to their mission of environmental protection?

To address this, Patagonia made a bold move.

The Net-Positive Move Patagonia Made

Their now-famous "Don't Buy This Jacket" campaign wasn't just clever marketing – it was a direct challenge to the fast-fashion mentality. The campaign encouraged customers to consider repairing their existing gear instead of buying new items, perfectly aligning with Patagonia's environmental ethos. Alongside this, they doubled down on using recycled materials, launched their "Worn Wear" program to facilitate gear repair and resale, and committed to donating one percent of their sales to environmental causes. These weren't isolated efforts – they were a cohesive strategy to ensure their operations reflected their mission.

Patagonia's results have been as impressive as their audacity. By 2022, they reported that 87 percent of the materials used in their products were recycled, a significant step toward reducing their environmental footprint. Their Worn Wear program has gained traction globally, proving that customers value brands that help them extend the life of their purchases. Even the "Don't Buy This Jacket" campaign, which might have seemed like a sales killer, ultimately boosted brand loyalty and positioned Patagonia as a leader in purpose-driven business.

Of course, the journey wasn't without its challenges. Patagonia faced scrutiny from skeptics who questioned whether their bold messaging was simply a marketing ploy. Additionally, achieving high percentages of recycled materials required years of innovation and collaboration across their supply chain. They learned that transparency was their best ally; by openly sharing both their wins and their struggles, they built trust and credibility with their customers.

Patagonia's story shows that being bold and authentic can set a business apart in powerful ways. Whether it's a groundbreaking campaign or a simple policy shift, the lesson here is that every action should authentically reflect your purpose. And while not every company can adopt such sweeping initiatives overnight, Patagonia proves that taking meaningful steps, no matter how small, can have a lasting impact.

If there's one takeaway from Patagonia's approach, it's this: sustainability isn't a static goal – it's a continuous journey. Whether you're exploring recycled materials, extending product life, or donating to causes that align with your mission, the key is to stay committed to the work. Every step forward strengthens your brand, engages your customers, and moves you closer to net-positivity.

Case Study 3: Buffer – Pay Transparency and Equitable Benefits

For Buffer, a midsize social media management company, building a purpose-driven business wasn't just about their product – it was about taking care of their team. As a fully remote company with employees spread across the globe, they faced the challenge of fostering trust and equity within a diverse workforce while staying competitive in the tech industry.

The Net-Positive Move Buffer Made

Buffer's net-positive move was groundbreaking: they implemented pay transparency, publishing all employees' salaries – including those of the leadership team – on their website. This bold step wasn't just a PR move; it was a tangible commitment to fairness and accountability. They also adopted a transparent formula for calculating salaries, considering factors such as cost of living, experience, and role, ensuring everyone was compensated equitably regardless of location.

Beyond pay, Buffer invested heavily in employee benefits. They introduced a minimum vacation policy, ensuring employees took at least three weeks off per year, and offered generous parental leave regardless of gender. They also covered 100 percent of health insurance costs for employees and their families, demonstrating that they valued their team's well-being as much as their productivity.

Buffer's efforts have already yielded impressive results, proving that a commitment to equity and transparency can drive both employee satisfaction and business success. Employee satisfaction scores consistently rank above industry averages, and the company has one of the highest retention rates in its sector. Their transparency has not only built trust internally but also externally; customers often cite Buffer's commitment to equitable practices as a reason for choosing their platform.

Buffer's pay transparency initiative inspired similar efforts across the tech industry, proving that smaller companies can lead meaningful change. By sharing their formula and process publicly, they helped other businesses understand how to create fair and equitable compensation structures.

Here are some other noteworthy examples:

- **Basecamp – open salaries and transparent career ladders:** Basecamp introduced a transparent salary formula and published it for their team, ensuring employees understood how their compensation was calculated. This initiative not only clarified expectations but also removed ambiguity about pay, fostering trust and fairness within the company.

- **GitLab – remote work transparency:** As a fully remote company, GitLab publicly shares its employee handbook, which includes policies on pay, promotions, and work expectations. By making their processes open, GitLab empowers both employees and external stakeholders to understand how they operate, setting a new standard for transparency in the tech space.

- **Salesforce – equal pay for equal work:** Salesforce made headlines for committing $16 million to close its gender-pay gap over several years. By conducting regular pay audits and adjusting salaries as needed, the company demonstrated that achieving pay equity is an ongoing commitment.

- **Kickstarter – public benefit corporation and employee advocacy:** Kickstarter transitioned to a Public Benefit Corporation (PBC) to ensure that social impact remained at the core of its mission. The company also empowers its employees through collective bargaining, showing that equitable pay and benefits go hand in hand with sustainable purpose-driven operations.

- **Reddit – pay equity through the elimination of negotiation:** In an effort to reduce gender and racial pay disparities, Reddit eliminated salary negotiations for new hires. Instead, they standardized starting salaries based on roles and levels, removing biases that often disadvantage underrepresented groups.

These examples highlight how tech companies, both small and large, are stepping up to tackle equity and transparency. By sharing their methods and outcomes, these businesses create a chain of events that inspire others across the industry to prioritize fairness, inclusion, and accountability.

But back to Buffer.

Of course, their path to success wasn't without hiccups. When Buffer first published its salary data, some employees felt vulnerable, worried that their compensation would be scrutinized by friends or family. To address this, Buffer invested in one-on-one conversations with team members to explain the benefits of transparency and to ensure they felt supported.

Another challenge came with balancing pay equity and cost of living. While transparency improved fairness, employees in high-cost areas sometimes struggled with the formula's limitations. Buffer addressed this by introducing cost-of-living adjustments to ensure all employees could thrive in their respective locations.

So, what can you take away from Buffer's journey?

It starts with a willingness to ask hard questions about how your organization supports its people. Are your team members paid fairly? Do they have access to meaningful benefits that enhance their well-being? By investing in your people, you create a culture where employees feel valued, engaged, and aligned with your mission.

In creating a culture of fairness and trust, you'll not only build a stronger team but also strengthen your brand as a business that truly cares. Buffer proves that midsize businesses can lead the way in purpose-driven practices, and their success shows that caring for your team is not just good ethics – it's good business.

Case Study 4: Ben & Jerry's – Social Justice Meets Ice Cream

How does an ice cream brand become a leader in social justice? Ben & Jerry's understood early on that their business couldn't just sprinkle activism on top like a topping – it needed to be fully baked into their operations, values, and public voice. They faced the question many brands do: how to balance profits with standing up for controversial issues, all while maintaining the trust of their customers and stakeholders.

The Net-Positive Move Ben & Jerry's Made

Ben & Jerry's made social justice central to their operations and brand identity. They committed to using 100 percent Fair Trade Certified ingredients, ensuring ethical sourcing and fair wages for farmers. But they didn't stop there. The company became an outspoken advocate for causes such as racial equity, LGBTQ+ rights, and climate justice.

In 2016, they publicly supported the Black Lives Matter movement, releasing a powerful statement that resonated globally. Their activism goes beyond statements – they back up their words with action by funding grassroots organizations (such as the Center for Popular Democracy and Color of Change) and engaging their supply chain to reflect their values.

This combination of delicious products and unapologetic purpose resonated with their audience, proving that businesses can – and should – have a voice in social justice.

What has Ben & Jerry's progress been like to date?

Ben & Jerry's impact is evident in both their operations and advocacy:

- **Fair Trade certification:** the company sources 100 percent Fair Trade Certified cocoa, sugar, vanilla, coffee, and bananas, directly benefiting small-scale farmers worldwide.

- **Climate commitments:** Ben & Jerry's became a certified B Corporation and committed to becoming net-zero by 2050, aligning their business with global sustainability goals.
- **Amplifying marginalized voices:** through campaigns such as "Justice ReMix'd," they've partnered with organizations working to reform the criminal justice system, making their stores and products a platform for change.
- **Customer engagement:** their activism hasn't alienated customers – instead, it's fostered loyalty. Sales continue to grow as their values align with those of socially conscious consumers.

While Ben & Jerry's has achieved significant progress in aligning their business with their social justice values, the journey hasn't been without hurdles. They've faced criticism and controversy for their outspoken stances, and balancing bold activism with business operations required careful navigation. Yet, these challenges became opportunities for growth, teaching the company how to stay true to its mission while building resilience and deepening trust with its community.

- **Facing backlash:** Ben & Jerry's bold stance on issues such as Black Lives Matter drew criticism from certain groups. However, the company stood firm, recognizing that authenticity would strengthen their connection with their core audience.
- **Balancing advocacy and operations:** while their activism garners headlines, staying consistent across their supply chain and sustainability efforts required ongoing investment and vigilance.
- **Avoiding performative activism:** unlike some brands accused of "virtue signaling," Ben & Jerry's lessons include the importance of taking concrete actions – such as donations, partnerships, and operational changes – backing their words with real impact.

These challenges taught Ben & Jerry's that standing for something often means standing in the fire. But it's worth it when your mission aligns with your customers' values and the broader good.

The main takeaway here is not about the scale of their efforts but the consistency of their commitment. You don't need to launch nationwide campaigns to start integrating purpose into your business. Maybe it's about sourcing ethically, partnering with a local nonprofit, or simply sharing your values authentically with your audience.

Start small but aim big.

What's one issue that aligns with your mission and matters deeply to your customers? Take a stand, make a plan, and build from there.

Final Scoop (Pun Intended)

Ben & Jerry's shows us that purpose-driven business isn't just about selling products; it's about selling a vision for a better world. They've proven that when you connect your operations, advocacy, and values, you don't just win customers – you build a movement. Whether you're scooping out ice cream or launching a new product, it's never too early – or too late – to start making an impact.

From My Experience: The Power of Incremental Wins

When I first started integrating purpose into my work, I fell into the trap of thinking every initiative had to be massive. What I've learned? Incremental wins build momentum. For example, in one project, we implemented a simple sustainability audit that revealed easy wins, such as switching to digital reports instead of printing thousands of pages annually. The cost savings funded bigger initiatives down the line.

Start small, celebrate wins, and build from there.

Transformation doesn't happen overnight – it's a marathon, not a sprint.

Each of the companies (case studies) noted in this chapter had different challenges, goals, and strategies, but they all share one thing in common: a commitment to aligning purpose with action. And their efforts paid off, creating measurable impact for their businesses, their communities, and the planet.

These stories prove that whether you're a multinational corporation or a small business, the journey to becoming net-positive is worth it. It's not about being perfect; it's about progress, persistence, and purpose.

Ready to apply these lessons to your own industry?

In Chapter 10, we'll explore how to tailor net-positive strategies to your business type. Whether you're in retail, tech, nonprofit, or government, you'll discover actionable insights to take your purpose-driven vision to the next level.

Let's turn these lessons into strategies that work for you.

KEY TAKEAWAYS

Action over theory
This chapter highlights businesses that turned purpose into tangible results, showing that no matter your size, aligning actions with values leads to impactful outcomes.

Case study lessons:

- IKEA
- Patagonia
- Buffer
- Ben & Jerry's

Progress, not perfection
Each organization faced challenges but used setbacks as opportunities to adapt, demonstrating that incremental wins build momentum for greater transformation.

Start small, aim big
You don't need to be a global giant to begin. Small, meaningful steps can lay the foundation for lasting change.

10

Sector Spotlights

Tailoring Strategies for Your Business Type

What do a tiny mom-and-pop bakery, a billion-dollar tech giant, and a government sustainability program have in common? More than you think.

Take this story, for example: Smallhold, a Brooklyn-based mushroom farming startup, launched in 2017 with the vision of making sustainable agriculture scalable. Their high-tech, vertical farming methods were designed to use less water, produce less waste, and bring fresh mushrooms closer to consumers. Investors flocked to support their mission, and for a while, Smallhold was a sustainability success story.

But by 2024, the company had shut down its farms, laid off staff, and filed for bankruptcy. The problem? Despite a strong purpose and brand, their business model relied heavily on venture capital and expensive technology, rather than ensuring long-term financial stability.

When profitability targets weren't met fast enough, Smallhold's funding dried up, proving that even the best sustainability intentions can collapse without a solid strategy.

On the other end of the spectrum, Microsoft made headlines when it announced its carbon-negative goal – promising to remove more carbon than it emits by 2030. The company poured billions into climate innovation, created internal carbon taxes, and pushed sustainable policies that transformed not just its own operations, but its entire industry.

The impact? Massive.

The lesson? Purpose-driven strategy can work at any scale – but it must be backed by a financially viable plan.

So, whether you're running a nonprofit, managing a small business, leading a corporation, or shaping government policy, the question isn't if the **Net-Positivity Framework** applies to you. It's how.

This chapter is your roadmap. We're not talking about a one-size-fits-all approach. We're diving into real-world, sector-specific strategies that indicate how businesses and organizations – big and small – are turning purpose into measurable impact. And just so you know, we'll also debunk a few myths along the way (like the idea that sustainability is only for big-budget corporations – spoiler alert: it's not).

No matter your industry, you have the power to build a net-positive business.

The secret? Tailoring the right strategies to fit your world.

By now, you're probably sold on the **Net-Positivity Framework** (or at least curious enough to keep reading – thanks for that!). But you might also be wondering: *how does this apply to me? My business isn't Patagonia or Ben & Jerry's. We're a nonprofit, or a small family-run café, or maybe even a government office. Does this really work for everyone?*

Spoiler alert, again: it does!

The beauty of the **Net-Positivity Framework** lies in its adaptability.

Whether you're running a tech startup in Silicon Valley, managing a nonprofit in a small town, or overseeing a government department, the principles of purpose, operations, measurement, and leadership can scale and shift to fit your unique context.

This chapter is your personalized playbook. We're going deep into tailored strategies that address the specific challenges and opportunities in four key sectors: nonprofits, small businesses, corporations, and government organizations.

Oh, and fair warning: this chapter includes a little tough love, a lot of practical advice, and a few "if they can do it, so can you" moments.

Let's jump in!

Nonprofits: Mission in Action

Nonprofits wear purpose on their sleeves, but let's be honest – sometimes that passion for the mission can lead to a bit of chaos. Ever heard of "mission creep?" It's what happens when you try to chase every opportunity, grant, or partnership that sounds even remotely aligned with your cause. Suddenly, you're juggling ten priorities, and none of them are getting the attention they deserve. Enter the **Net-Positivity Framework** – a way to focus on measurable impact while keeping your organization rooted in its purpose.

Challenge #1: Chasing Funding Without Losing Focus

Let's face it, grants and donations often come with strings attached. I've worked with organizations that shifted their focus entirely to chase a big grant – only to realize a year later that they were completely off mission. Don't let that be you. Use your purpose as a filter: does this funding align with your core goals? If not, it's okay to say no.

How to Stay Focused

- Create a strategic plan and stick to it.
- Develop diverse funding streams, so you're not overly reliant on one big grant or donor.
- Communicate your "why" clearly to funders. The right partners will fund your mission, not try to steer it.

As a former Executive Director of the Oregon Zoo Foundation, I saw firsthand how tricky corporate partnerships can be, especially when sponsors come to the table wanting maximum visibility for relatively modest investments. One of the strategies I focused on was ensuring that every corporate partnership had a clear connection to our purpose. For example, Asian elephants have long been a cornerstone of the zoo's mission, and the challenges we face in preserving their future perfectly illustrate how aligning mission-driven work with corporate sponsorships can lead to impactful, long-term partnerships.

When corporate sponsors initially approached us, many were eager to fund high-visibility projects, such as flashy elephant exhibits, to showcase their brands prominently on zoo grounds. While these offers were tempting, they often didn't align with our broader conservation goals, which extended far beyond the zoo itself to include global efforts such as rewilding Asian elephants and protecting their natural habitats. To ensure that these partnerships supported both parties, we reframed the conversation: how could their sponsorship help save an endangered species while still meeting their goals for visibility and impact?

For instance, instead of simply branding an exhibit, we proposed a partnership that focused on the zoo's work in rewilding Asian elephants and addressing human-elephant conflict in Southeast Asia. Through this collaboration, corporate partners could fund conservation education programs, visitor engagement activities, and field research that would directly support efforts to protect wild populations. Sponsors gained visibility by having their logos featured in storytelling campaigns that highlighted their role in making these efforts possible – think documentary-style videos shown in the zoo, interactive exhibits, and community outreach materials.

One example of this alignment was creating an educational campaign centered on the importance of wildlife corridors for elephants. The campaign not only brought attention to the critical role these corridors play in reducing human-elephant conflict, but it also included branding opportunities at key touchpoints for the sponsor. This way, corporate partners didn't just fund an exhibit – they became an integral part of a larger narrative about global conservation efforts, fostering a sense of purpose and pride.

Lessons Learned

1. **Elevate the mission:** Asian elephants provided a clear, compelling purpose that resonated with sponsors and visitors alike. By focusing on the larger mission of species survival, we shifted the conversation from "what can we offer you?" to "how can we make a difference together?"
2. **Create tangible impact:** sponsors valued knowing their support was contributing to real-world conservation outcomes, such as rewilding efforts or funding field teams working on habitat restoration in Southeast Asia. Communicating these tangible impacts made the partnerships more meaningful and enduring.
3. **Engage sponsors in the work:** beyond branding, we invited corporate partners to participate in the conservation journey. This included exclusive opportunities to meet field researchers, host employee volunteer days tied to conservation efforts, and even co-sponsor global summits focused on wildlife conservation.

Whether you're working with Asian elephants or advocating for another cause close to your heart, the key is aligning your mission with your partners' goals. By crafting partnerships that go beyond transactions and deeply involve your sponsors in the mission, you can achieve remarkable outcomes – both for your organization and the species or communities you aim to protect. It's not just about visibility; it's about creating meaningful impact, one partnership at a time.

Challenge #2: Limited Resources and Overworked Teams

In nonprofits, "doing more with less" feels like the job description. I've seen it firsthand – teams trying to save the world with duct tape budgets and endless passion. The problem? Burnout is real, and it's hard to stay mission-focused when your team is stretched thin.

I know it's a cliché, but it's true: working smarter, not harder, is the secret sauce for nonprofits and purpose-driven organizations. The challenges – tight budgets, limited staff, and the ever-present pressure to deliver impact – mean you can't afford to waste time or resources. Success comes from focusing on strategies that amplify your mission and maximize every dollar spent. Let's break it down:

- **Leverage partnerships for greater reach:** no one can tackle big challenges alone, and you shouldn't have to. Collaborating with like-minded organizations or businesses lets you pool resources, share expertise, and multiply your impact. Take Feeding America, for example: they work with grocery stores to rescue millions of pounds of food that would otherwise go to waste. It's a win-win partnership that reduces hunger while addressing food waste – a mission-aligned collaboration at its finest.

    In my experience as CEO of Big Brothers Big Sisters of Central Florida, partnerships were pivotal. When we merged smaller independent organizations into a single entity with regional reach across five counties, collaboration became our lifeline. It wasn't just about economies of scale – it was about amplifying our ability to serve more kids with better resources. We also built a statewide coalition to advocate for school-based mentoring, securing a line item in the state's Department of Education budget. Partnerships weren't just helpful – they were transformational.

- **Use metrics to prioritize efforts:** data is your best friend when it comes to working smarter. By tracking the social return on investment (SROI), you can identify which programs deliver the most impact per dollar spent. For nonprofits especially, this is invaluable in showing funders and stakeholders where their money is making the biggest difference.

  For example, during my time as Executive Director at the Peninsula Family YMCA, a branch of the YMCA of Greater San Francisco, we faced a challenging but crucial decision. The Y had a reputation for running a wide array of programs, but the reality was that not all of them were creating the level of impact we aspired to achieve. We had to take a hard look at what was working and what wasn't, using tools such as social return on investment (SROI) to analyze the true value of each initiative.

Ultimately, we made the strategic decision to consolidate multiple lower-impact programs and double down on three high-impact ones that directly aligned with our mission of youth development, healthy living, and social responsibility. The result? We were able to serve more families, improve the quality and outcomes of our programs, and give our team the resources and focus they needed to do their best work.

By prioritizing impact over sheer volume, we not only strengthened our connection with the community but also gained the trust of funders who saw that their contributions were making a meaningful difference. This approach reinforced a critical lesson: focusing on quality over quantity isn't just better for your bottom line – it's better for the people you serve.

Lessons Learned
1. **Clarity is key:** merging organizations requires a crystal-clear mission and defined goals to avoid mission creep.
2. **Data drives decisions:** SROI and other metrics weren't just buzzwords – they were essential tools for proving our value to funders and stakeholders.

3. **People power the mission:** we focused on building strong teams and empowering staff, which was critical during the transition and beyond.

Whether you're leading a nonprofit, managing a business, or building community programs, the lesson is simple: work smarter by focusing on what matters most. Build partnerships that amplify your mission. Use data to make informed decisions. Streamline your efforts to do fewer things better.

You don't have to overhaul everything at once – start small. Identify one program, partnership, or process you can optimize and take it from there. Working smarter isn't just about efficiency; it's about creating the greatest possible impact with the resources you have.

Challenge #3: Attracting and Retaining Top Talent

Nonprofits can't always compete with corporate salaries, but they have one big advantage: purpose. People want to work where they feel they're making a difference. The trick is to make sure your organization is a place where employees feel valued, heard, and aligned with the mission.

How to Be a Talent Magnet

- Offer growth opportunities such as leadership training or certifications.
- Build a culture of transparency and trust – people thrive when they understand how their work contributes to the mission.
- Emphasize work-life balance. Passion doesn't mean 24/7 availability.

Challenge #4: Proving Impact to Donors and Stakeholders

Donors love a good story, but they love data even more. Vague claims such as "we made a difference" won't cut it anymore. In today's world, donors and stakeholders expect clear, measurable outcomes that validate their investment. This isn't about adding charts to your annual report;

it's about weaving data into your storytelling to create a compelling, transparent narrative that builds trust and attracts long-term support.

Ways You Can Turn Metrics into Magic

1. **Pair stories with data:** use tools such as social return on investment (SROI) to demonstrate the ripple effect of your work, supported by testimonials that show its human impact.
2. **Share transparent impact reports:** include photos, stories, and data points in reports or newsletters to create a holistic view of your work.
3. **Highlight measurable progress:** break down specific goals and showcase how your organization is achieving them step by step.

For example, during my tenure as Senior Executive Director of Philanthropy at the YMCA of San Francisco, we faced a challenge common to many nonprofits: how to shift from merely delivering services to providing outcomes. The programs we offered were impactful, but we needed a way to demonstrate this to donors in a way that resonated deeply.

We transitioned to an outcome-based service delivery model, redefining our programs to focus on measurable success. For example, instead of reporting that "50 families participated in our healthy living program," we tracked and shared outcomes like, "90 percent of families improved their eating habits and reduced screen time by an average of two hours per day."

To communicate this transformation, we developed a marketing campaign with a strategic cadence that tackled the challenge of proving our impact head-on.

- **Pose the challenge:** we started each campaign by framing a relatable issue for our audience, such as childhood obesity or limited access to after-school programs.

- **Offer our solution:** we highlighted specific programs, such as a youth fitness initiative or family wellness workshops, using two stories to show the human side of our work – families who improved their health, and children who discovered a love for exercise.
- **Present the data:** each campaign included a standout statistic, such as, "75% percent of participants maintained their healthy lifestyle changes six months after completing the program."
- **Make the "call to action":** we invited donors to be part of the solution, urging them to support initiatives that directly addressed these challenges.

This approach brought in more than just financial support – it deepened donor relationships and created advocates for our mission. It also highlighted the importance of transparency, as we weren't afraid to share areas where we still needed to improve.

Another Example of Proving Impact: Heifer International

Organizations such as Heifer International have perfected this model. They don't just talk about providing livestock; they quantify how their support lifts entire communities out of poverty. A single goat, for instance, can provide milk for a family to sell, fund education, and create lasting financial stability. By detailing these outcomes and pairing them with personal stories, Heifer has established itself as a global leader in proving nonprofit impact.

You don't need a global campaign to start proving your impact. Begin with one program. Track measurable outcomes. Share a story. Pair it with a data point. Then invite your supporters to make the next chapter of the story possible.

This strategy isn't just about showcasing results – it's about inspiring your donors and stakeholders to feel like an integral part of your mission's success.

Running a nonprofit is tough – you're balancing passion with practicality, juggling limited resources, and constantly proving your worth to donors. But here's the good news: you don't have to do it all at once. Start small. Identify one area where you can use the **Net-Positivity Framework** – whether it's tracking metrics, engaging your team, or refining your funding strategy – and build from there.

Your mission is the heart of your organization, but data, partnerships, and focus are your muscles. Together, they can turn your nonprofit into a powerhouse of purpose and impact.

Show the world what you're capable of.

Small Businesses: Big Impact on a Smaller Scale

Small businesses might not have the deep pockets or extensive resources of Fortune 500 companies, but they hold an incredible advantage: agility, authenticity, and a personal connection to their communities. Your size isn't a limitation – it's your superpower. You can pivot faster, respond directly to customer feedback, and build trust in ways that larger corporations often struggle to replicate.

Start small, think big.

You don't need to overhaul your operations overnight to make an impact. Start with small, values-driven changes that resonate with your mission and scale as you grow.

For example, a neighborhood coffee shop could:

- Switch to compostable cups and reusable straws.
- Source coffee beans from Fair Trade Certified suppliers.
- Highlight these changes in their branding to engage eco-conscious customers.

In my own small business, Hera Associates, one of our clients was a local, family-owned boutique bakery with a heartfelt mission to serve their community. Like many small businesses, they were grappling with operational challenges while yearning to address a growing issue in their city: homelessness. Every day, they watched the news and saw how more families were being displaced, with shelters and food banks struggling to meet demand. At the same time, they faced a dilemma – unsold baked goods and perfectly edible pastries and breads were being thrown away. It was a stark contrast that didn't sit well with them. They reached out to us, determined to turn this waste into a way to combat food insecurity and support their neighbors in need.

Together, we developed a plan that not only tackled food waste but directly addressed the rising homelessness crisis in their community.

Here's how it came to life:

- **Partnering with purpose:** the bakery partnered with a local homeless shelter that provided meals for families and individuals experiencing homelessness. By connecting with the shelter, we ensured that every unsold croissant, muffin, and loaf of bread went to those who needed it most. The shelter director shared that these baked goods added a sense of comfort to meals that were often purely functional.
- **Logistics that worked:** a major challenge was ensuring the food was still fresh when it reached the shelter. We coordinated a simple pick-up schedule, where volunteers from the shelter collected donations each evening. This streamlined approach minimized disruption to the bakery's operations and ensured their goods made it to dinner tables in time.
- **Amplifying the message:** to build momentum, the bakery let customers know their purchases were part of something bigger. Signs in the shop proudly stated, "Our muffins help fight hunger in our community," and social media posts showcased the direct impact of their donations. Photos of smiling shelter volunteers carrying boxes of pastries resonated deeply with the bakery's customers.

- **Engaging the community:** we introduced quarterly "Bake for Good" events where customers could sponsor additional baked goods for donation. This allowed people to participate directly in the mission, creating a bridge between the bakery, their customers, and those in need.

The impact of this initiative was far-reaching:

- **Reduced food waste:** the bakery cut its waste by 60 percent in just the first month, diverting hundreds of baked goods from the landfill.
- **Support for local shelters:** over the course of a year, the bakery's donations provided snacks and desserts for over 2,000 meals at the shelter.
- **Increased customer engagement:** customers rallied behind the cause. One regular customer commented, "It's great knowing that my morning coffee and scone help support a bigger mission."
- **Boosted sales:** the bakery's transparency and purpose-driven marketing attracted new customers. Over six months, they saw a 12 percent increase in sales.

Of course, the journey wasn't without its challenges. Initially, there were concerns about liability and food safety, common fears for small businesses entering food donation programs. We worked with the bakery to understand local food donation laws and implemented staff training on handling donations properly. They also learned that clear communication with the shelter was vital to avoid donating items that couldn't be used effectively.

The biggest lesson? Purpose is contagious.

The bakery staff felt more connected to their work, customers became advocates, and the community saw a local business stepping up to address a pressing issue.

For this bakery, addressing food waste wasn't just a nice idea – it became a lifeline for their community and a rallying cry for their customers.

It's proof that small businesses have the power to tackle big issues, starting right where they are.

If you're a small business owner, ask yourself: *what's a challenge facing my community that aligns with my business's values?*

Whether it's donating unsold products, hosting fundraisers, or partnering with local nonprofits, you create meaningful change.

Your unsold muffin could become someone else's fresh start. And in a world where homelessness is on the rise, that's a purpose worth serving.

And in case my client example wasn't enough for you, we can look at Sweetgreen as a success story.

Sweetgreen started as a single, modest salad shop in Washington, D.C., with an ambitious goal: to make healthy, sustainable food accessible to everyone. What began as a local eatery founded by three college friends in 2007 has since transformed into a national brand, proving that small businesses can scale purpose alongside profit.

Local Sourcing: Building Relationships with Farmers

From its inception, Sweetgreen prioritized sourcing ingredients from nearby farms, a commitment that not only supported local agriculture but also ensured fresh, seasonal produce in every bowl. This approach required building strong, trust-based relationships with farmers and navigating the challenges of scaling without sacrificing quality.

As Sweetgreen expanded to over 200 locations, they maintained this core value by creating regional supply chains tailored to local farming communities. For example, in California, Sweetgreen works with small-scale organic growers to source avocados, while in the Northeast, they partner with family-run dairy farms for cheese. By staying connected to the communities they serve, Sweetgreen's local sourcing strategy has set a standard for sustainability in fast-casual dining.

Transparent Impact Reporting: Making Sustainability Visible

Sweetgreen understands that customers care about where their food comes from and how it impacts the planet. Early on, the company began tracking its environmental footprint, implementing initiatives such as composting kitchen scraps, reducing packaging waste, and choosing energy-efficient lighting and appliances in their locations.

Sweetgreen shares these efforts transparently with customers, publishing annual sustainability reports and using their website to highlight their progress. For example, in 2022, Sweetgreen announced that they had diverted 40 percent of their waste from landfills through composting and recycling programs. They also committed to achieving carbon neutrality by 2027, a goal they openly track and update their customers on.

Community-Building: Beyond the Salad Bowl

Sweetgreen's purpose extends beyond serving healthy meals – it's about creating experiences that foster a sense of community. Early on, they began hosting "Sweetlife" music festivals, combining their love for food, music, and sustainability. These events featured performances from major artists while promoting eco-friendly practices like reusable water bottles and waste separation stations.

As the company grew, they pivoted to wellness workshops, in-store events, and partnerships with schools to promote nutrition education. For instance, their "Sweetgreen in Schools" program teaches children about the importance of healthy eating and sustainable agriculture, turning their purpose into a tangible, hands-on experience for the next generation.

Scaling Purpose without Sacrifice

As Sweetgreen scaled from one location to more than 200 nationwide, they faced the inevitable challenge of maintaining their mission while growing rapidly. Instead of diluting their purpose for efficiency, Sweetgreen leaned into it as a differentiator. They invested in technology to ensure seamless supply chain management and partnered with local nonprofits to stay connected to the communities they serve. Their app, for instance, not only makes ordering easy but also highlights the local farms supplying ingredients for each bowl. Customers know exactly where their kale, quinoa, or tomatoes came from – a feature that builds trust and loyalty.

Sweetgreen's purpose-first approach has not only resonated with customers but it has also driven measurable success:

- **Customer loyalty:** their transparency and commitment to sustainability have fostered a devoted customer base. Many customers cite Sweetgreen's values as a primary reason for choosing their meals over competitors'.
- **Financial growth:** in 2021, Sweetgreen became a publicly traded company; a milestone that underscored its ability to scale purpose alongside profit.
- **Community impact:** through programs such as "Sweetgreen in Schools," they've reached over 35,000 students, teaching them the importance of nutrition and sustainable food systems.

Sweetgreen's story proves that small businesses can lead with purpose and still grow exponentially. The key is staying true to your mission while embracing innovation and building trust with your community.

If you're a small business owner, ask yourself:

- How can I support local producers or suppliers?
- What sustainable practices can I implement to reduce waste or emissions?
- How can I build deeper connections with my customers and community?

You don't need a national presence or a massive budget to make a difference. Sweetgreen's journey started with one restaurant and a simple belief: food should do good. Your business can start small, too – one sustainable practice, one community partnership, and one inspired customer at a time.

As they say, the journey of a thousand miles begins with a single step – or in this case, a single compostable cup.

Let your actions speak, and your impact will grow.

Corporations: Scaling Purpose for Profit

Corporations operate under a microscope. With vast resources come immense opportunities – but also heightened responsibility. Customers, employees, and investors are demanding that corporations balance profit with impact. Whether it's addressing sustainability, equity, or community engagement, the stakes are high, and the **Net-Positivity Framework** offers a roadmap to navigate this pressure with authenticity and success.

Imagine a global company like yours becoming not just a market leader but a purpose leader. It's not about PR spin; it's about building a legacy that aligns scale with impact. And let's be honest – if you're not steering the ship toward purpose, you might just find yourself sinking under public scrutiny or outpaced by competitors who are.

So how do corporations effectively scale purpose across every department?

It starts with embedding mission-driven strategies into the DNA of your operations, ensuring that every team contributes to a unified goal. Purpose can't just live in your corporate social responsibility (CSR) department – it must permeate everything. From sustainable sourcing in procurement to equitable messaging in marketing, your entire organization needs to walk the talk.

Take Unilever again as a shining example of this. Their Sustainable Living Plan integrates purpose into every product line.

Dove focuses on body positivity; Lifebuoy champions global hygiene; Knorr invests in sustainable agriculture.

This integration isn't just feel-good – it drives profitability by resonating with consumers and aligning with future-focused investors.

To truly embed purpose into your organization, start by taking a hard look at how each department aligns with your mission. Imagine your company as a symphony: every section – from procurement to HR to marketing – needs to play its part in harmony with your purpose. For instance, procurement might evaluate whether the materials you source are ethically and sustainably produced. This could mean choosing Fair Trade Certified suppliers or investing in renewable resources. HR, on the other hand, could take steps to ensure equitable hiring practices by broadening outreach to underrepresented communities or implementing bias training for recruiters.

Purpose-driven initiatives don't stop at alignment – they should also tie directly to what your business does best. For example, a tech company might overhaul its supply chain to prioritize renewable energy sources or develop products designed to reduce energy consumption. Consider Google's commitment to carbon neutrality, which includes ensuring that every byte of data processed is offset by renewable energy. Not only does this strategy align with their mission, but it also reinforces their role as an industry leader in sustainability.

For any business, the key is to start small and scale up. Maybe your first step is reviewing supplier contracts to ensure they meet ethical standards, or perhaps you begin by training managers to foster inclusive team environments. Every step you take reinforces your commitment to aligning operations with your purpose – and it signals to your employees, customers, and stakeholders that you're serious about walking the talk.

But ingraining purpose is just the beginning. To truly lead with impact, corporations need to back up their initiatives with transparent data that builds trust and engage their employees to champion the mission from within.

Let's explore how these elements can turn a purpose-driven strategy into measurable, scalable success.

Use Data to Build Trust

Metrics don't just measure progress – they validate it. When you share transparent data about your purpose-driven goals, you're building trust with stakeholders.

Look at Salesforce and its annual sustainability report. Salesforce doesn't just say they're committed to net-zero emissions; they show it. Their publicly available data demonstrates their progress and invites stakeholders to hold them accountable, turning transparency into a competitive advantage.

What you can do
- Develop a reporting cadence that shares your purpose metrics with customers, employees, and investors.
- Leverage tools such as the Global Reporting Initiative (GRI) or SASB Standards to standardize your reporting.

Empower Employees as Advocates

Your employees are your secret weapon in scaling purpose. When you engage them in meaningful initiatives, they'll amplify your mission organically.

Google's Green Team is a brilliant example. This employee-led initiative develops innovative ideas to reduce the company's carbon footprint, such as hosting internal hackathons to design energy-efficient data centers. By empowering employees, Google doesn't just reduce emissions – it fosters innovation and loyalty.

What you can do
- Create a purpose-driven task force or ambassador program for employees passionate about sustainability or equity.

- Reward purpose-driven initiatives with internal recognition or funding for employee-led projects.

Microsoft's "AI for Earth" program is an inspiring example of how a corporation can align its purpose with its strengths to tackle some of the world's biggest challenges. It's a reminder that the tools and talents already at your disposal can create massive impact when applied thoughtfully. Whether it's combating climate change or creating a more equitable world, success begins with leveraging what you do best.

But here's the thing: it's not just about grand gestures or billion-dollar budgets. It's about authenticity and follow-through. Think of it like making a promise to your friends or family – if you say you're going to show up, you better mean it. The same is true in business. Customers, employees, and stakeholders are looking to see if your actions match your words.

What can you learn from Microsoft?

It's not just their scale or their funding that sets them apart – it's their ability to weave purpose into the very fabric of their business strategy. They didn't launch AI for Earth as a side project; they made it an extension of their core expertise in technology, ensuring that it's deeply connected to their identity.

And here's the best part: you don't have to be a tech giant to follow their lead. Whether you're running a regional logistics company or a national retail chain, the same principle applies: align your purpose with your strengths. By doing what you already do well – but with purpose – you can amplify your impact and inspire trust.

What's your AI for Earth?

It might not involve advanced algorithms or global initiatives, but there's something your business excels at that could create a domino effect. Maybe it's your ability to connect people, deliver products sustainably, or champion diversity in your field. The point is to start where you are and let authenticity guide the way.

And let's be real: customers are savvier than ever. They can spot a hollow "green" label or a purpose-washing campaign from a mile away. If you're going to promise sustainability or equity, you need to back it up with action. So, invest in genuine practices – whether it's reducing emissions, building an inclusive workplace, or giving back to your community.

The reward? Stronger trust, deeper loyalty, and a legacy that lasts.

When corporations lead with purpose, the impact isn't just felt within their walls. It ripples outward – to employees, communities, and even the planet.

And the best part? You don't have to choose between profit and purpose. When you align the two authentically, they fuel each other.

Now is the time to ask yourself: *how can my business drive the kind of change that matters?* Because when you get it right, the results are transformative – not just for your bottom line, but for the world we all share.

Governments: Leading by Example

Government organizations wield a unique and powerful influence. Their policies, investments, and public initiatives not only serve communities directly but also set the tone for businesses and citizens. In the movement toward net-positivity, governments have the opportunity – and the responsibility – to lead by example, driving widespread change and inspiring collective action.

Governments are the architects of public life. Their decisions shape everything from infrastructure and education to healthcare and environmental policy. Adopting net-positive strategies can transform these systems to benefit both people and the planet. It's not just about doing good – it's about improving trust, efficiency, and long-term resilience. And let's face it: in an era where citizens demand accountability and sustainability, governments can't afford to lag.

But there's more to it.

When governments lead with purpose, they set the stage for businesses to follow suit. Policies that incentivize green practices or prioritize equity ripple outward, influencing corporate behavior and empowering citizens to act. It's a win-win: public institutions fulfill their mandate to serve, while private enterprises and individuals gain a clear path to contribute to societal well-being.

Tailored Strategies for Government Organizations

Prioritize Green Infrastructure

Governments have unparalleled reach when it comes to shaping communities through infrastructure. By investing in projects such as renewable energy, water conservation, and urban reforestation, public leaders can lay the groundwork for sustainable living.

For example: in Portland, Oregon (where I happen to be sitting as I write this chapter!) the "Green Roofs" program is a standout initiative that illustrates how cities can tackle climate challenges while enhancing urban livability. Launched as part of the city's broader sustainability goals, the eco-roof requirement in the Central City 2035 plan incentivizes buildings to install vegetation-covered rooftops through tax credits, grants, and development bonuses. These green roofs, which replace traditional roofing materials with layers of soil and plants, provide a host of benefits that ripple through the community.

- **Environmental benefits:** green roofs play a vital role in stormwater management, capturing rainfall and reducing runoff that can overwhelm sewer systems. In a city known for its wet climate, this has significantly mitigated flooding risks. Additionally, these rooftops combat urban heat by insulating buildings and cooling the surrounding air, which helps reduce the "heat island effect" in densely built areas. By improving air quality and supporting biodiversity, Portland's green roofs also serve as minihabitats for pollinators and other wildlife.

- **Economic incentives:** the program is designed to make adoption financially attractive for property owners. Building owners who install green roofs often benefit from reduced energy costs due to improved insulation, as well as extended roof lifespans, since the vegetation shields roofing materials from harsh weather and UV exposure. These savings, combined with city-offered financial incentives, have driven widespread uptake in both residential and commercial buildings.
- **Social impact:** beyond environmental and economic gains, Portland's green roofs program has created community pride and engagement. Some buildings have transformed their rooftops into community gardens or gathering spaces, fostering connections among neighbors. The program has also inspired other cities to follow suit, with municipalities across the United States studying Portland's success to develop their own green infrastructure initiatives.

Lessons for Other Governments

Portland's green roofs program is a model for how cities can create scalable solutions to climate challenges that offer tangible benefits to businesses, residents, and the environment. By combining regulation, financial incentives, and public education, the city has made sustainability an accessible and appealing choice for property owners. This approach underscores how governments can lead by example and demonstrate that green initiatives are not just environmentally essential but also economically and socially rewarding.

Foster Equity in Public Services

Governments are tasked with ensuring that public programs serve all residents equitably. When equity becomes a cornerstone of public policy, it elevates entire communities, particularly marginalized groups.

Los Angeles' electric bus initiative is a compelling example of how environmental progress can go hand in hand with social equity.

Recognizing the urgent need to reduce greenhouse gas emissions and improve urban air quality, the city launched an ambitious program to transition its public transit system to 100 percent zero-emission electric buses by 2030.

But the initiative goes beyond simply adopting greener technology – it prioritizes inclusivity and accessibility for all residents, ensuring that sustainability efforts benefit everyone, particularly underserved communities.

- **Environmental impact:** the transition to electric buses is a critical component of Los Angeles' broader climate goals. With public transit buses accounting for a significant portion of urban emissions, the city's adoption of zero-emission vehicles is expected to drastically cut carbon dioxide and nitrogen oxide levels. This change will have a profound impact on air quality, especially in neighborhoods near heavily trafficked transit corridors, which are often home to low-income families disproportionately affected by pollution-related health issues like asthma and cardiovascular disease.

- **Social equity focus:** what sets this initiative apart is its commitment to inclusivity. Los Angeles has integrated accessibility improvements into the rollout of its electric bus fleet, ensuring that the transit system better serves all residents, including people with disabilities. The new buses are equipped with state-of-the-art features such as lower floors for easier boarding, wider aisles to accommodate wheelchairs, and advanced communication systems to assist visually and hearing-impaired riders. Additionally, the city has prioritized electrifying routes that serve communities historically burdened by environmental injustices. These areas often experience higher rates of pollution and lack access to reliable, affordable transportation. By focusing on these neighborhoods first, Los Angeles is addressing systemic inequities while making sustainable transit more accessible to everyone.

- **Economic and operational benefits:** the electric bus initiative is also a win for the local economy. Transitioning to electric buses has created new jobs in vehicle manufacturing, charging infrastructure development, and fleet maintenance. The city has partnered with local suppliers to source buses, keeping investment within the region and bolstering the local economy. Moreover, electric buses have lower operating and maintenance costs compared to traditional diesel buses, which will save the transit authority millions of dollars in the long term.

Implementing such a large-scale initiative hasn't been without its hurdles.

Early challenges included the high upfront cost of electric buses and charging infrastructure, as well as the need to retrain drivers and maintenance staff. To address these issues, Los Angeles leveraged state and federal funding programs, including grants from the Federal Transit Administration, and partnered with private companies to share the financial burden.

The city also conducted extensive community outreach to ensure buy-in from residents and advocacy groups. Public forums, surveys, and educational campaigns helped demystify the new technology and showcased the dual environmental and social benefits of the initiative.

Los Angeles' electric bus initiative offers a roadmap for other cities looking to align sustainability goals with social equity. It proves that environmental progress doesn't have to come at the expense of inclusivity – it can enhance it. By prioritizing accessibility, addressing environmental justice, and building partnerships to overcome financial barriers, Los Angeles is leading by example.

Engage Citizens in the Process

Government initiatives succeed when communities feel involved. Transparency, collaboration, and citizen input build trust and ensure that programs meet real needs.

New York City's "PlaNYC" initiative is a shining example of how bold vision and public engagement can drive meaningful change. Launched in 2007, PlaNYC was born out of a simple but powerful idea: to prepare the city for a sustainable and equitable future in the face of growing urban challenges such as climate change, population growth, and aging infrastructure.

What sets PlaNYC apart is its comprehensive approach, combining ambitious environmental goals with strategies to enhance livability and foster economic growth, all while actively involving the public every step of the way.

PlaNYC has set ambitious targets that tackle some of the city's most pressing challenges:

- **Reducing greenhouse gas emissions:** the city committed to reducing its carbon emissions by 30 percent by 2030. To achieve this, PlaNYC introduced policies to retrofit buildings for energy efficiency, expand green energy usage, and reduce vehicle emissions through initiatives like bike-sharing and pedestrian-friendly zones.
- **Increasing energy efficiency:** recognizing that buildings account for nearly 70 percent of the city's emissions, PlaNYC implemented energy benchmarking and retrofitting programs for both residential and commercial properties. Incentives such as tax breaks encouraged landlords to adopt sustainable upgrades.
- **Improving quality of life:** PlaNYC isn't just about the environment – it also prioritizes health, equity, and livability. From planting over a million trees through the "MillionTreesNYC" initiative to expanding waterfront parks and affordable housing, the program strives to make New York a better place for all residents.

As someone who considers Brooklyn to be my forever home, even though I moved away from the city in 2005, I can attest to the tremendous changes in public green spaces and people-focused developments. On every visit back, I'm amazed at how areas that were once concrete jungles have transformed into vibrant, welcoming spaces where families gather, communities thrive, and nature feels a little closer. It's a testament to the power of bold vision and persistent action.

What makes PlaNYC a "masterclass in public engagement" is the way it has invited New Yorkers to be active participants in shaping and implementing the plan.

Here's how:

- **Citizen advisory boards:** local advisory groups were established to provide input, represent diverse communities, and hold the city accountable. These boards ensure that the needs and concerns of residents – from environmental justice to affordable housing – are heard and addressed.
- **Public progress reports:** PlaNYC takes transparency seriously. Regularly published reports track progress on its goals, allowing residents to see what's been achieved and where more work is needed. This level of accountability builds trust and fosters a sense of shared ownership over the city's future.
- **Community workshops and town halls:** the initiative hosted hundreds of public events to gather feedback, educate residents, and inspire grassroots action. Whether it was brainstorming sessions on local park designs or workshops on reducing household energy use, these events connected the city's vision with everyday lives.

PlaNYC's impact has been nothing short of transformative:

- **Carbon emissions:** by 2022, New York City had reduced its greenhouse gas emissions by 20 percent, making substantial progress toward its 2030 target. Programs such as "Local Law 97," which mandates emissions reductions in large buildings, have been instrumental.

- **Tree planting:** the MillionTreesNYC initiative surpassed its goal ahead of schedule, planting 1.2 million trees and increasing the city's green cover, which helps combat urban heat islands and improve air quality.
- **Energy efficiency:** over 500,000 buildings have undergone energy efficiency upgrades, significantly lowering the city's overall energy consumption.

Of course, PlaNYC has had its fair share of obstacles.

Early on, skepticism about the feasibility of such ambitious targets created pushback from some stakeholders. Funding these large-scale initiatives also required creative financing solutions, such as public-private partnerships and green bonds. One key lesson was the importance of clear communication: when residents understand how projects directly benefit them – such as cleaner air, lower energy bills, or safer streets – they're more likely to support them.

Another challenge was balancing priorities. Expanding green spaces and bike lanes sometimes faced opposition from neighborhoods concerned about gentrification and displacement. The city responded by engaging communities early in the planning process and pairing green initiatives with affordable housing investments.

As a business owner, taxpayer, or resident, PlaNYC demonstrates the power of collective action. It's a reminder that when governments lead with bold vision and involve their communities, transformative change is possible. For businesses, supporting and aligning with these initiatives can enhance your impact and reputation – whether through green building practices, participating in community projects, or adopting sustainable operations that align with local goals.

For citizens, PlaNYC shows how your voice matters. By staying informed, participating in advisory boards, or attending town halls, you can help shape the policies that directly affect your community. PlaNYC isn't just a city government success story – it's a testament to what's possible when an entire community comes together to tackle challenges and create a shared vision for the future.

Why This Matters: Connecting Government to Businesses and Citizens

The relationship between government, businesses, and citizens is symbiotic. Public policies set the stage for private innovation, and engaged communities amplify the impact of government initiatives. When governments adopt net-positive strategies, they lead by example, encouraging businesses to step up and citizens to support transformative change.

Think about it: when a local government installs electric vehicle charging stations, it helps reduce emissions while making EVs more practical for businesses and families. When public programs prioritize accessibility, it creates a workforce that's healthier, happier, and more inclusive. These efforts create a ripple effect that benefits everyone.

Governments have the power to model the world we want to live in. Their policies shape not just the present but the possibilities for the future. For public leaders, the mandate is clear: lead with purpose and watch as businesses, communities, and individuals rise to the occasion. Because when governments prioritize sustainability, equity, and transparency, they don't just serve their citizens – they inspire them.

What's Next: Tailored Tools for Your Sector

No matter your sector, the **Net-Positivity Framework** is adaptable, scalable, and – most importantly – actionable. The key is to start where you are, use the strategies that make sense for your context, and commit to continuous improvement.

In Chapter 11, we'll explore how to keep the momentum going. From building resilience to adapting strategies as your business evolves, this next chapter will ensure your net-positive journey is built to last.

Let's sustain the impact you're creating – and take it to the next level.

KEY TAKEAWAYS

Adaptability for all

The Net-Positivity Framework works across sectors – nonprofits, small businesses, corporations, and governments – by tailoring purpose-driven strategies to fit unique challenges and opportunities.

Nonprofits:
- Avoid "mission creep" by aligning funding and partnerships with your core goals.
- Use data and storytelling to prove impact and attract donors.
- Focus on staff well-being and sustainability to prevent burnout.

Small businesses:
- Leverage agility and local connections to make small, impactful changes (e.g., sourcing locally, reducing waste).
- Build purpose into customer engagement and community partnerships.

Corporations:
- Align purpose with core business strengths for scalable impact.
- Use data transparency to build trust and empower employees as advocates.
- Balance profitability with sustainability and equity.

Governments:
- Lead by example through green infrastructure, equity-focused policies, and community engagement.
- Foster collaboration between public policies, businesses, and citizens to amplify impact.

11

Staying the Course

Long-Term Planning and Adaptability

Picture this: a CEO walks into an all-hands meeting and drops a bombshell. "In five years," he announces, "this company won't exist as we know it today. We're tearing it all down." Employees exchange uneasy glances.

Did they just hear their boss announce their impending unemployment?

However, instead of panic, the room buzzes with something else – curiosity. Because this wasn't just any CEO. It was Paul Polman, the then-CEO of Unilever, one of the world's largest consumer goods companies. And he wasn't talking about shutting down the company – he was talking about completely rebuilding it.

At the time, Unilever was a global powerhouse, selling everything from ice cream to shampoo. But Polman saw the writing on the wall. The world was changing. Resources were depleting. Consumer trust was shifting. And if Unilever wanted to stay the course, it couldn't keep operating the way it always had. So, he launched the Unilever Sustainable Living Plan – an ambitious strategy to cut the company's environmental impact in half while doubling its profits.

It was a bold, risky move. Investors balked. Shareholders worried. Analysts scoffed. But Polman stayed the course, refusing to be swayed by short-term pressures. Over the next decade, Unilever proved the skeptics wrong. The company grew faster than its competitors, attracted top talent, and became a leader in corporate sustainability.

The lesson? Staying the course doesn't mean standing still. It means adapting, evolving, and making decisions that secure long-term impact – even when the world (or your investors) pushes you to play it safe.

In this chapter, we'll explore how to build resilience, pivot when necessary, and ensure your net-positive strategy isn't just a flash in the pan but a lasting, impactful force. Because no matter how well you plan, the road ahead won't be a straight line. There will be detours, storms, and unexpected twists. The key isn't avoiding change – it's learning how to navigate it.

Imagine you've just planted a beautiful garden. You've tilled the soil, chosen the right seeds, and given it the care it needed to thrive. But what happens if you stop watering, forget to pull weeds, or fail to adapt to changing weather? The garden you've worked so hard to cultivate – your net-positive business – won't just stagnate; it will wither. Neglect leads to overgrowth in some areas, drought in others, and ultimately, a loss of the balance and vibrancy that made it thrive in the first place.

Just like a garden, a business rooted in purpose and impact requires constant care. Watering is akin to nurturing your strategies and relationships. Pulling weeds represents removing inefficiencies or obstacles. And adapting to changing weather mirrors adjusting to market trends, economic shifts, or global challenges.

Think about the unexpected – an economic downturn, a shift in customer expectations, a global pandemic, or a technological breakthrough.

Without resilience and adaptability built into your approach, these changes can feel like an unrelenting storm. However, when you're prepared to adjust your strategies and tend to your foundation, you ensure that your garden not only survives but thrives through any season.

Maintaining your impact strategy isn't just a once-a-year commitment; it's a daily practice. It requires regularly assessing what's working, what's not, and what's growing in unintended directions. Just like adding compost to enrich soil or rotating crops to maintain fertility, your business needs periodic reinvestment, innovation, and a willingness to pivot when necessary. By treating your impact strategy as a living, breathing system, you'll ensure it flourishes for years to come.

Welcome to the heart of sustainability: staying the course. This is where you'll find out what it takes to maintain momentum in your net-positive journey. Spoiler alert: it's not about coasting once you've hit your first milestone. It's about building resilience, learning to pivot, and staying aligned with your goals while adapting to inevitable changes.

The Journey, Not the Destination

Net-positivity isn't a box to check off – it's a mindset. It's about committing to continuous improvement, not perfection. The world changes, markets shift, and priorities evolve. The key is to build a business model that can weather those changes and come out stronger on the other side.

Take Patagonia, a company we've visited a few times throughout this book. This brand has been a beacon of sustainability for decades, consistently proving that purpose and profit can coexist. But their success isn't rooted in rigid plans or static strategies. Patagonia thrives because it embraces adaptability and continuous improvement.

When research revealed that microplastics from recycled materials – one of Patagonia's cornerstones of sustainability – were making their way into oceans, the company didn't shy away from the problem. Instead of abandoning recycled materials altogether, they doubled down on innovation.

Patagonia invested in research to mitigate microplastic shedding and collaborated with industry experts to push for systemic solutions, such as improved washing machine filters and material science breakthroughs.

Their commitment to their mission – protecting the planet – never wavered, but their strategies evolved to meet new challenges. They've also pivoted in other areas, such as transitioning to regenerative organic farming practices for cotton and expanding their activism to address broader climate justice issues.

The lesson here? What works today might need rethinking tomorrow, and that's not a failure – it's the hallmark of resilience. Businesses, like ecosystems, are dynamic. Patagonia's willingness to adapt has not only strengthened its brand but also reinforced its leadership in sustainability.

For you, this might mean reevaluating materials, reconsidering partnerships, or shifting focus based on emerging research or consumer feedback. Staying the course doesn't mean never changing direction – it means staying true to your mission while navigating the best path forward.

Building Resilience into Your Business Model

Every business will face challenges – economic downturns, supply-chain disruptions, shifts in consumer preferences, or even unexpected crises like pandemics. Resilience is your superpower to navigate these obstacles without losing sight of your purpose. But resilience doesn't just happen; it's built through intentional strategies that prepare your business to adapt, recover, and thrive in the face of change.

Here's how to build it:

Diversify revenue streams

Don't put all your eggs in one basket. Whether it's developing new products, tapping into untapped markets, or diversifying funding sources, a varied portfolio creates stability. For instance, during the pandemic, countless restaurants pivoted to offering meal kits and delivery services. One high-end restaurant in New York City, known for its in-person dining experience, began creating gourmet meal kits complete with video tutorials from the chef. This not only kept their business afloat but opened a new revenue stream they continue to use today. The lesson? Flexibility in how you generate income can make the difference between surviving and thriving during uncertain times.

During my time as Senior Executive Director at the YMCA of San Francisco, I experienced firsthand the power of resilience and adaptability during the pandemic. Overnight, 60 percent of our earned business revenue disappeared as mandatory shutdowns brought our programs and services to a halt. It was a moment of reckoning: how could we keep the organization afloat while addressing the unprecedented challenges facing our community?

We didn't have all the answers immediately, but we started with a simple question: what do we have, and how can we use it to serve? The YMCA owned several facilities that now sat empty due to closures, and we had a wealth of expertise in childcare, youth services, and well-being. With those assets in mind, we pivoted – leaning into our strengths and reimagining how we could leverage them for the greater good.

The first critical need was clear: first responders and emergency workers had to stay on the job to keep our communities safe. But with schools and daycares shuttered, how could they work without reliable childcare? Partnering with local governments, we quickly retooled some of our facilities to provide emergency childcare for first responders.

Thanks to emergency funding from government agencies, we were able to offer these services free of charge to all first responders and emergency service workers. This funding not only eliminated barriers for families who needed the support most but also allowed us to sustain limited operations at the YMCA.

As the pandemic dragged on, another pressing issue emerged: many children, especially those from underprivileged backgrounds, lacked access to the resources needed for remote learning. They didn't have quiet spaces, reliable Wi-Fi, or adult support to navigate online schooling. Recognizing the growing educational divide, we took action.

Once again, with the support of government partnerships and funding, we transformed more of our facilities into socially distant learning centers. Equipped with our staff's expertise, the YMCA provided children with the space, technology, and guidance they needed to succeed in virtual school. This initiative didn't just bridge a digital divide – it leveled the playing field for children who might otherwise have fallen through the cracks.

This experience reinforced an essential truth: resilience comes from leveraging your strengths in innovative ways. By focusing on what we could offer – our facilities, staff expertise, and community trust – and combining that with strategic partnerships and funding, we not only sustained the YMCA through one of the toughest periods in its history but also served as a cornerstone of support for the community.

It wasn't easy. There were logistical challenges, funding gaps, and moments of uncertainty. But by aligning our resources with urgent community needs and securing the financial support required to deliver those services, we built new partnerships, strengthened our reputation, and fulfilled our mission in ways we hadn't imagined before.

The YMCA's response to the pandemic offers a powerful blueprint for resilience:

- **Assess your assets:** what resources, expertise, or partnerships can you leverage in times of change?
- **Focus on immediate impact:** align your efforts with the most pressing needs of your community or customers.
- **Collaborate for sustainability:** build partnerships that bring funding, expertise, or scale to your initiatives.

- **Embrace innovation:** don't be afraid to retool your operations or try new approaches. Sometimes, the most impactful solutions come from thinking outside the box.

This approach doesn't just apply to nonprofits like the YMCA. Whether you're a small business, a corporation, or a government agency, the principles remain the same: start with what you have, identify what's needed, and adapt to meet the moment.

And as someone who's lived this firsthand, I can promise you: it's not just about surviving – it's about discovering new ways to thrive. When you lean into your purpose, adapt with intention, and partner with others to amplify your efforts, your organization can emerge from any challenge stronger than before.

What could this look like for your business? A small retail shop could add an online store to reach customers beyond its local area. A nonprofit might diversify funding sources by exploring corporate sponsorships or developing fee-for-service programs. The key is to identify new opportunities that align with your mission while adding stability to your financial foundation.

Invest in "Scenario Planning"

Scenario planning isn't about predicting the future – it's about being prepared for it. Think of it as playing chess with potential challenges: you're not just reacting to what happens but anticipating moves, risks, and opportunities several steps ahead. This strategic foresight enables businesses to navigate disruptions without losing momentum, ensuring they stay agile and focused on their purpose.

Consider this: what happens if raw material prices suddenly spike? If new regulations upend your industry? If a competitor launches a game-changing product that eats into your market share? Without a plan, businesses are left scrambling, making reactive decisions that often fall short. With scenario planning, you're ready to respond with confidence and clarity.

Let's take another look at REI, the outdoor retailer known for its commitment to sustainability and outdoor adventure. Scenario planning is baked into their operational strategy, allowing them to assess risks ranging from the impacts of climate change on outdoor recreation to evolving consumer behaviors.

When the pandemic hit, REI's preparedness paid off. They quickly pivoted to prioritize digital sales, focusing on e-commerce and curbside pickup. Their marketing shifted as well, emphasizing messages that resonated with customers seeking solace in nature. As other retailers struggled to adapt, REI's foresight allowed them to not only survive but thrive, maintaining their reputation as a trusted brand for outdoor enthusiasts.

Their proactive approach extended beyond sales: REI reevaluated its supply chain to mitigate disruptions and leaned into partnerships with conservation organizations, reinforcing their brand identity. Scenario planning gave them the agility to adapt to short-term challenges while staying aligned with their long-term mission.

Scenario planning is a tool that businesses of all sizes can leverage.

Here's how to start:

- **Identify potential scenarios:** begin by brainstorming "what if?" questions specific to your business. What if your top supplier suddenly shuts down? What if your customer base shifts toward digital-only engagement? What if the cost of transportation doubles due to new fuel regulations?
- **Develop response strategies:** for each scenario, outline potential responses. If a key supplier shuts down, could you establish a backup supplier relationship? If transportation costs spike, could you localize your supply chain or optimize delivery routes?
- **Create financial models:** build projections for different economic conditions. For instance, how would a ten percent increase in raw

material costs affect your margins? What changes would you need to make to maintain profitability?
- **Engage your team:** scenario planning isn't a solo exercise. Involve cross-functional teams to bring diverse perspectives to the table. Employees on the front lines often have insights into risks and opportunities that leadership might overlook.

Let's take my example from the YMCA mentioned above to see how scenario planning played out in real time.

During my time at the YMCA of San Francisco, we used this strategy to navigate the unprecedented challenges of the pandemic by asking tough "what if?" questions: What if shutdowns extended for months? What if donor funding dried up? What if community needs drastically changed? Those "what ifs" became the foundation for decisive action that not only helped us survive but also allowed us to serve our community in ways we had never imagined.

The answers to these questions led to innovative solutions, such as transforming our facilities into emergency childcare centers and socially distant learning hubs. By preparing for worst-case scenarios, we turned a dire situation into an opportunity to serve the community and sustain the organization.

Scenario planning isn't about predicting doomsday scenarios – it's about building confidence and resilience. It gives you the ability to act swiftly and strategically when the unexpected happens. Think of it as a safety net for your business, ensuring you can adapt to challenges without losing sight of your long-term goals.

Even if you're a small business owner, asking simple "what if?" questions can uncover vulnerabilities and opportunities you hadn't considered. And when you combine this foresight with purpose-driven decision-making, you're setting yourself up to thrive, no matter what the future holds.

Foster a Culture of Innovation

Innovation isn't just about creating the next big thing – it's about empowering your team to think creatively and solve problems in new ways. Google's famous "20% Time" policy, which allows employees to spend one-fifth of their time on passion projects, has led to innovations such as Gmail and Google Maps. While not every company can afford such a generous policy, the principle remains the same: give your people the freedom to explore ideas and experiment.

Consider Brooks Brothers, the iconic American clothing manufacturer. During the early days of the COVID-19 pandemic, Brooks Brothers faced a sharp decline in demand for its traditional business attire, as workplaces shifted to remote environments. Instead of sitting idle, the company pivoted to meet a pressing societal need: the production of personal protective equipment (PPE).

Here's how they turned a challenging situation into a success story:

Fostering innovation and adaptability

Brooks Brothers repurposed their production lines, normally used for creating dress shirts and suits, to manufacture face masks and gowns for healthcare workers and essential personnel. This pivot required rethinking every part of their operations, from sourcing materials suitable for medical-grade PPE to retraining employees to produce entirely new products.

While this move didn't immediately replace the revenue lost from declining suit and dress-shirt sales, it allowed the company to keep its factories running and retain workers who might have otherwise faced layoffs. Employees felt a renewed sense of purpose, knowing their work directly contributed to public health during a global crisis. This effort boosted morale and demonstrated the company's commitment to both its workforce and its community.

Brooks Brothers' pivot wasn't just a temporary fix; it reinforced their reputation as a company that adapts to meet the moment. The goodwill generated during the crisis strengthened their brand loyalty and opened the door to partnerships with government agencies and health organizations. The shift also showcased their ability to innovate, positioning them as a company prepared to weather future challenges.

For small manufacturing companies, this example highlights the value of an innovative mindset and agile leadership.

Here's how you can apply similar principles:

- **Encourage employee input:** Brooks Brothers listened to their workers' ideas and involved them in the transition, fostering a collaborative and empowered culture.
- **Leverage existing resources:** the company used its existing facilities and expertise to pivot quickly, showing that innovation doesn't always require new investments.
- **Align with market needs:** identifying a growing demand for PPE during the pandemic ensured their pivot was both impactful and sustainable.

The lesson here is clear: no matter the size of your business, fostering a culture of adaptability and innovation can help you navigate challenges and even uncover new opportunities. Ask yourself: *what are my company's strengths, and how can they be repurposed to meet a changing market need?* The answer could lead to solutions that sustain your business and inspire your team.

Resilience is the backbone of your business's ability to stay the course and fulfill your mission, even when the road gets bumpy. By diversifying your revenue streams, anticipating challenges through scenario planning, and fostering a culture of innovation, you'll build a business that can weather storms, adapt to change, and come out stronger on the other side.

Your ability to thrive in uncertainty will also inspire confidence in your employees, customers, and stakeholders, reinforcing your commitment to a purpose-driven and sustainable future.

Ask yourself: *what steps can I take today to future-proof my business?*

Resilience starts with intentional choices, and the time to start is now.

Regular Reviews: Your Net-Positive Check-Up

Let's face it: even the best-laid plans don't always go perfectly, and that's okay. Regular reviews are your chance to pause, reflect, and adjust before small missteps become major roadblocks. Think of these check-ins as your business's annual physical or routine oil change – they're not glamorous, but they're essential. They catch issues early, highlight progress, and help you stay aligned with your mission. Plus, they're an opportunity to celebrate wins (because who doesn't love a good milestone celebration?).

Consistency is key when it comes to maintaining momentum. Whether you choose to review quarterly, biannually, or annually, stick to a schedule that works for your company's size and pace.

For example, at Patagonia, leadership conducts quarterly reviews of their sustainability initiatives. These sessions allow teams to share updates on their progress toward ambitious goals, such as reducing their carbon footprint and improving supply chain practices. By checking in regularly, they can pivot quickly when challenges arise, such as supply shortages or regulatory changes.

For your business, start with a simple framework:

- What's going well?
- What's not working?
- What needs to change before the next review?

Evaluate KPIs

Metrics are your compass in the net-positive journey. During reviews, don't just glance at your KPIs – dig deep. Are you hitting your targets? If not, why? Maybe a supplier isn't meeting sustainability expectations, or a new product isn't resonating with customers. Use your data to make informed decisions and refine your approach.

Imagine a coffee company with a goal to source 100-percent Fair Trade Certified beans by 2026. During a biannual review, they discover one supplier isn't meeting standards. Instead of scrapping the goal, they identify alternative suppliers and develop a transition plan. This kind of proactive evaluation keeps the company on track while maintaining transparency with stakeholders.

Engage Stakeholders

Let's be honest – sometimes you're too close to the problem to see the solution. That's where feedback from your team, customers, and partners becomes invaluable. Regular reviews should include input from these groups, offering fresh perspectives that can reveal blind spots or inspire new ideas.

For example, Salesforce, known for its commitment to sustainability and equity, involves employees in their quarterly reviews. They've created internal forums where teams can suggest improvements to their environmental or DEI initiatives. One suggestion – a shift to more energy-efficient office spaces – came directly from an employee working on their facilities team and resulted in significant cost savings and a smaller carbon footprint.

For your business, consider hosting review workshops or anonymous surveys to gather feedback. Questions like, "What's one area where we could improve our impact?" or "What's a recent success we should scale?" can spark meaningful dialogue.

Regular reviews aren't just about finding faults – they're about staying accountable and adaptable. They're your chance to course-correct when things go off track, double down on what's working, and ensure everyone remains aligned with your mission. And remember: these check-ins don't have to feel like a chore. Frame them as opportunities to celebrate progress, involve your team in strategic thinking, and recommit to your purpose.

In the end, a thriving, net-positive business isn't one that never stumbles – it's one that consistently learns, evolves, and moves forward with intention. Think of your reviews not as just meetings but as meaningful milestones on the road to lasting impact.

Adaptability

Adaptability isn't just a buzzword – it's the cornerstone of long-term success. Let's dive into a few examples that highlight how embracing change, rather than resisting it, has set iconic companies on a path to resilience and growth.

LEGO – Their Journey to Sustainability

LEGO is a beloved household name, with its iconic plastic bricks cherished across generations. But even a giant like LEGO recognized the need to adapt in the face of growing environmental concerns. In 2015, the company made a bold announcement: a $150-million investment to replace its traditional plastic bricks with sustainable materials by 2030.

As inspiring as that mission was, the journey has been far from smooth. Midway through their efforts, LEGO encountered a significant technical challenge – recycled materials weren't durable enough to meet the company's rigorous standards for strength, safety, and vibrant colors. For a brand built on quality and creativity, compromising these values wasn't an option.

Instead of shelving their ambitious goal, LEGO did what every resilient company should: they adapted. By extending their timeline and doubling down on research, the company made strides in material science. By 2022, they successfully produced prototypes made from sustainable materials, bringing them closer to their mission while maintaining the integrity of their product.

LEGO's story teaches us that adaptability is about persistence and flexibility. Challenges are inevitable, but how you respond to them can define your legacy.

Adaptability isn't just about responding to problems – it's about preparing for them. The most successful companies don't just react to change; they anticipate it, see it as an opportunity, and act boldly.

Netflix – Reinventing the Way We Watch

Take Netflix, for example. The company launched in 1997 as a DVD rental service – a business model that, by today's standards, feels like ancient history. Customers would order DVDs online and wait for them to arrive by mail, and while it was innovative for its time, the model had its limitations. Recognizing the potential of emerging streaming technology and the growing demand for on-demand content, Netflix made a daring pivot in 2007 to a subscription-based streaming service.

That bold move didn't just save the company; it revolutionized the entertainment industry. Netflix foresaw the decline of physical media and capitalized on the shift toward digital consumption before its competitors could. But they didn't stop there. Netflix doubled down on their adaptability by venturing into original content production in 2013, starting with *House of Cards*. It was a gamble – after all, they were going head-to-head with established studios – but it paid off. Today, Netflix produces hundreds of original series, movies, and documentaries, from *Stranger Things* to *The Crown*, becoming a global powerhouse in entertainment.

Netflix's transformation didn't just keep them relevant – it made them a cultural phenomenon. Today, they're synonymous with binge-watching and original content – seriously, who hasn't lost a weekend to "just one more episode?" (I know I have!) This adaptability shows how a company can move from being good to truly extraordinary, proving that the ability to anticipate and embrace change is one of the greatest strengths a business can have.

Ford – Driving into the Future

Ford, another pioneer of adaptability, has taken bold steps to redefine the auto industry for a sustainable future. Known for its legacy in gasoline-powered vehicles, Ford recognized the need to pivot as consumer demand for greener alternatives surged. Their introduction of the F-150 Lightning, an electric version of their iconic truck, marked a significant milestone. The Lightning combines the rugged reliability Ford is known for with cutting-edge electric technology, offering features such as the ability to power homes during outages – a nod to real-world utility.

Beyond developing EVs, Ford has invested heavily in the infrastructure needed to support this shift. Partnerships with companies such as Electrify America and BlueOval Charging Network are paving the way for a robust, accessible EV charging ecosystem. The company has also committed billions to building dedicated EV manufacturing facilities, such as the BlueOval City mega-campus in Tennessee, which aims to produce next-generation batteries and electric vehicles.

Ford's embrace of autonomous technology is equally ambitious. By partnering with tech leaders and investing in self-driving systems, Ford is preparing for a future where vehicles are not only electric but also autonomous. These strategic moves highlight the company's commitment to not just keeping pace with industry changes but leading them.

The result? Ford is evolving from an automaker to a future-focused mobility company – proving that even a century-old brand can adapt, innovate, and thrive in the face of disruption.

***

In each case – LEGO, Netflix, and Ford – these companies didn't just survive challenges; they thrived by leaning into change. They didn't view obstacles as roadblocks but as opportunities to innovate and stay relevant.

So, how can you build this kind of resilience in your own organization? Start by embracing the mindset that change is inevitable, and your response to it matters more than the change itself.

Here are a few actionable steps:

- **Stay curious:** keep an eye on industry trends, consumer behavior, and emerging technologies. The earlier you spot potential shifts, the easier it is to adapt.
- **Empower experimentation:** foster a culture where testing new ideas is encouraged. Whether it's a new product line or an operational tweak, small experiments can lead to big breakthroughs.
- **Be transparent:** when challenges arise, communicate openly with your team and stakeholders. Admitting setbacks, as LEGO did, builds trust and shows a commitment to your mission.
- **Invest in learning:** scenario planning, like the one we used during my time at the YMCA, can help you anticipate disruptions and develop proactive strategies.

The world doesn't stand still – and neither should your business. Whether you're building a product as timeless as LEGO bricks or trying to revolutionize how people watch TV, adaptability isn't just a survival tactic; it's the key to thriving.

As you chart your net-positive journey, remember that setbacks aren't failures – they're opportunities in disguise. Lean into change, stay true to your purpose, and be ready to evolve. Because, as these examples show, resilience and adaptability are superpowers.

As a leader, your ability to adapt and sustain your impact directly affects your team, customers, and stakeholders.

Think about the trust you build when you show consistency in your mission, even in the face of challenges.

Think about the inspiration you provide when you model resilience and innovation.

Your commitment to staying the course also sets the tone for your industry. Whether you're running a small business, a nonprofit, or a multinational corporation, your efforts ripple outward. Every adjustment you make, every lesson you learn, contributes to the growing movement toward net-positivity.

From Resilience to Leadership

By now, you've built the foundation for a net-positive business. You've aligned your vision, embedded purpose into operations, measured impact, and fostered collaboration. Staying the course is about taking those pillars and reinforcing them with adaptability and long-term planning.

In Chapter 12, we'll explore how you can step into the role of a leader who inspires others to follow your path. Because net-positivity isn't just about your business – it's about creating a world where purpose and profit thrive together.

Let's lead the way.

KEY TAKEAWAYS

Net-Positivity is a journey, not a destination

Maintaining a purpose-driven business requires continuous care, reassessment, and adaptability.

- Build resilience.
- Review regularly.
- Embrace adaptability.
- Lead with transparency.

12

Leading the Way
Becoming a Champion for Net-Positivity

In 2008, Starbucks was on the brink of disaster. Sales were plummeting, customer loyalty was waning, and Wall Street was predicting the company's demise. Enter Howard Schultz, the company's former CEO, who returned to leadership with one mission: to reignite Starbucks' purpose.

His first move? He shut down every single Starbucks store.

For an afternoon, baristas across the country paused their usual routine to focus on what truly mattered – reconnecting with the company's core values. Schultz saw that Starbucks had become too focused on rapid expansion and financial growth at the expense of quality and culture. The brand wasn't just about coffee; it was about community, connection, and an experience. By taking a bold step – at great short-term financial cost – he made a statement: leadership isn't just about making profits. It's about making an impact.

The result? Schultz's leadership revival transformed Starbucks from a struggling chain into a global brand known for its ethical sourcing, social impact, and commitment to employees.

That's the difference between a manager and a leader. A manager fixes problems. A leader inspires change. A manager focuses on short-term gains. A leader builds a vision for the future.

If you're reading this, you're not here just to keep the wheels turning in your business. You're here to lead the way – to champion net-positivity in your organization, industry, and community. You don't need to shut down your entire operation like Schultz did, but you do need to make bold decisions that reinforce your purpose.

You're about to learn what it takes to move from simply managing a business to leading a movement – one that drives change, builds trust, and leaves a legacy.

The question isn't whether you can lead the way. The question is: are you ready to?

What's the difference between a good leader and a great one?

A good leader ensures their organization thrives. They're masters of the fundamentals: they organize, delegate, and problem-solve with precision. They communicate clearly, set expectations, and maintain stability even in challenging times. They focus on the task at hand, ensuring it's completed efficiently and effectively. Think of a good leader as the captain of a ship, expertly navigating through calm and stormy seas, ensuring everyone arrives safely.

A great leader, however, does more than steer the ship – they inspire the crew to dream of new horizons. They go beyond the basics, painting a vision that excites and energizes their teams. Where a good leader solves problems, a great leader empowers others to find solutions, fostering a culture of creativity and ownership. Where a good leader directs, a great leader connects – encouraging collaboration, listening deeply, and nurturing trust.

As the inspirational speaker on business leadership, Simon Sinek, said, "Leadership is not about being in charge. It is about taking care of those in your charge."

Let's be clear: becoming a champion for net-positivity doesn't mean standing on a soapbox shouting slogans (unless that's your thing, in which case, go for it). It's about influence, advocacy, and action. It's about inspiring others to see that purpose and profit aren't mutually exclusive – they're mutually reinforcing. And yes, it's about leaving your comfort zone and embracing the exhilarating, sometimes messy, often challenging journey of driving meaningful change.

If you've made it this far in the book, congratulations – you've already shown the mindset of a net-positive leader. You're not content with doing the minimum. You're ready to step into the transformative role of inspiring change, not just within your business but across your industry and community. Great leadership is about creating a ripple effect, where your actions spark others to rise to the occasion.

Take Microsoft under Satya Nadella's leadership as an example. Before Nadella, Microsoft was a solid company, but its culture was often described as rigid and competitive. Nadella didn't just refine operations; he reshaped the company's entire ethos. He fostered a culture of collaboration, learning, and purpose.

The result? Microsoft became not only more innovative but also more human – transforming from a good company to a great one that leads by example in both technology and sustainability.

Think of this as your call to greatness. Leadership is not just about managing the present; it's about envisioning the future and bringing others along for the journey. The question is, how can you elevate your leadership to inspire, empower, and create lasting impact? This chapter is your roadmap for doing just that. Together, we'll explore how to lead with vision, build trust, and advocate for change far beyond your office walls.

Great leaders don't just leave a legacy – they build one collaboratively with their teams, communities, and the world. So, if you're ready to move from managing tasks to inspiring transformation, let's dive in. The world is waiting for leaders like you.

Why This Matters (And Why It's Easier Than You Think)

Think about the leaders who've inspired you. Maybe it's a trailblazing entrepreneur like Patagonia's Yvon Chouinard, who turned sustainability into a brand cornerstone. Or perhaps it's someone closer to home – a boss who took the time to mentor you, a peer who pushed you to think bigger, or a community leader who rallied people around a shared mission.

Now, imagine being that person for someone else. That's the power of leadership. It's not about having all the answers; it's about inspiring others to ask the right questions, take action, and believe that change is possible.

The good news? You don't need a billion-dollar brand or a TED Talk to make an impact. You just need to start.

Advocacy in Action: Building Your Influence

Let's start with a simple truth: people follow people. If you want to inspire change, you need to lead by example. The following ways are how you can turn your influence into action.

Share Your Story

Stories are powerful. They're the way humans have connected, inspired, and driven change for millennia. A good story doesn't just inform – it moves people to action. Sharing your journey – the wins, the lessons, and the obstacles overcome – helps you connect with others in a way that spreadsheets and metrics simply can't.

Remember Patagonia? – a company we've visited throughout this book. Their campaigns, such as "Don't Buy This Jacket," weren't just clever marketing ploys – they were stories that resonated deeply with their audience. By explaining the environmental cost of consumerism and encouraging customers to repair rather than replace their gear, Patagonia didn't just sell jackets – they built a movement for mindful consumption. This story not only strengthened customer loyalty but also reinforced Patagonia's commitment to sustainability, positioning them as a global leader in purpose-driven business.

When I worked with the Anti-Defamation League (ADL), storytelling wasn't just an asset – it was the heartbeat of our mission. Fighting antisemitism, hate, and bigotry isn't something you achieve with data alone; you need stories that awaken empathy and inspire action. I remember one initiative where we shared the story of a student who had experienced bullying fueled by prejudice. Through ADL's anti-bias education programs, this student not only found support but became a leader in creating a more inclusive school environment.

By showcasing this transformation, we weren't just sharing a victory – we were demonstrating the tangible impact of our work. This approach not only motivated donors and educators to support our mission but also empowered others to become advocates for change in their own communities. Sharing these real-life stories built trust, mobilized resources, and reminded everyone involved why our work mattered so deeply.

- **Lessons from leaders**
  Howard Schultz, the former CEO of Starbucks, understood the power of storytelling in building a purpose-driven brand. During the company's rough patch in 2008, Schultz shared Starbucks' journey of transformation openly with employees and customers.

He talked about his commitment to reinvigorating the company's mission – to inspire and nurture the human spirit – by refocusing on quality, community, and sustainability. By sharing both the struggles and the path forward, Schultz rallied his team and strengthened Starbucks' bond with its customers.

- **How you can share your story**
  Your story doesn't have to be perfect – it just has to be real. Authenticity is what wins hearts and minds. Whether you're celebrating a big win or reflecting on a challenging setback, sharing your journey inspires others and builds trust. Here's how to start:
  - *Host a town hall:* gather your team or community and walk them through your journey. Highlight the purpose behind your work, share the hurdles you've faced, and celebrate the progress you've made.
  - *Write a blog post or newsletter:* share your experiences in a format that reaches your broader audience. For example, if you've made strides in reducing your company's carbon footprint, write about the process, the challenges, and the impact.
  - *Give a talk:* whether at an industry conference or a local community event, telling your story in person can make a profound impact. People remember stories they hear directly from the source.

You don't need to wait until you've achieved a massive milestone to share your journey. Begin by reflecting on a recent win or lesson learned. What challenges did you overcome? What impact have you seen? Frame it as a narrative that connects emotionally and inspires action. When you share your story, you're not just recounting your journey – you're inviting others to join it. And that's where real change begins.

Be a Connector

Change doesn't happen in a vacuum. It thrives in connection – the spaces where people with shared goals and values come together to amplify impact. Great leaders understand this and leverage their networks to build partnerships that achieve more than any one organization could alone.

Remember Howard Schultz, the former CEO of Starbucks? Let's look at how he exemplified the power of connection. Recognizing that student debt was a massive barrier for many employees, Schultz partnered with Arizona State University to create the "Starbucks College Achievement Plan." This program offers Starbucks employees full tuition coverage for online degree programs, changing the lives of thousands of workers while building loyalty and engagement. By connecting Starbucks' mission of nurturing the human spirit with a respected academic institution, Schultz created a win-win that inspired his team and elevated the brand.

Another example is Oprah Winfrey and the "Morehouse College Gift." Oprah Winfrey, one of the most influential connectors of our time, has long used her platform to bring people together for shared purpose. In 2019, Oprah announced a $13-million donation to Morehouse College, part of her ongoing commitment to providing scholarships for young men attending the historically Black college. But here's where it gets interesting – her gift wasn't just a financial transaction. Oprah leveraged her influence to rally other donors and media attention, creating a consequence that extended far beyond the initial donation.

Connecting people, organizations, and ideas has a multiplying effect. It's not just about linking resources; it's about fostering collaboration that builds trust, drives innovation, and creates lasting change. Research backs this up: a study by the University of Michigan found that organizations with high levels of collaboration were 5.5 times more likely to be high performing.

The power of collaboration isn't just theoretical – it's a proven driver of success.

But how do you make it happen?

Building meaningful connections doesn't require a massive network or endless resources; it starts with simple, intentional steps that bring people and organizations together for a shared purpose.

Here's how you can begin fostering connections that create lasting impact:

- **Identify shared goals:** look for overlap in missions, whether you're working with businesses, nonprofits, or community groups. What problem can you solve better together?
- **Facilitate introductions:** never underestimate the power of a well-timed introduction. If you know two organizations with complementary strengths, bring them together.
- **Co-host events or initiatives:** partner on a joint program, fundraiser, or community event that benefits both parties and strengthens your collective impact.

You don't need a massive platform like Oprah's to be a connector. Start by looking around your own community or industry. Who shares your values, and how can you work together? Whether it's teaming up with a local nonprofit for a community initiative or co-creating a product line with another business, small connections often lead to big results.

By being a connector, you're not just building bridges – you're creating pathways for shared success and purpose-driven change. And when people and organizations come together, that's when the magic happens.

Advocate Beyond Your Business

Let's get one thing straight: being a leader isn't just about running your organization – it's about stepping into the bigger arena and using your platform to make waves. Advocacy is your chance to move beyond your own walls and spark change in your industry, your community, and even the world. It's where you go from being a business leader to being a movement leader.

Take Ben & Jerry's as an example. These ice cream moguls don't just churn out Chunky Monkey – they churn out bold, unapologetic stances on social justice issues. From supporting Black Lives Matter to championing Fair Trade practices, Ben & Jerry's has used its brand as a megaphone for causes that matter.

The result? Sure, they've ruffled some feathers, but they've also built rock-solid loyalty among customers who admire their courage and values.

Now, you might be thinking: *but I'm not Ben & Jerry's!* That's okay. Advocacy doesn't mean you have to change the world overnight or grab a megaphone (unless you want to). It starts with showing up where it matters most.

Action Tip
Advocate with impact:

- **Join the conversation:** get involved with industry groups or community organizations that align with your mission. If you're in tech, join a green tech alliance. If you're in retail, advocate for sustainable supply chains.
- **Share your perspective:** write op-eds, post on LinkedIn, or give talks about the issues you're passionate about. Even a thoughtful blog post can spark a conversation that leads to change.
- **Show up for policy:** advocate for policies that drive systemic impact. Testify at local hearings, sign onto coalitions, or meet with lawmakers to share how proposed changes will benefit your industry and community.

Here's a challenge for you: think of one issue that keeps you up at night – whether it's environmental sustainability, equity in hiring, or access to education. Now, identify one way you can advocate for that issue beyond your business. Maybe it's sponsoring a panel discussion, rallying other businesses to join you, or even writing that op-ed you've been meaning to draft.

Advocacy in Action: A Story to Inspire

During my work with NYC homeless service reform, advocacy wasn't just a strategy – it was a lifeline for creating lasting change. In New York City, where the family shelter system was under immense pressure, Homes for the Homeless saw an opportunity to empower women living in shelters to become small business owners while addressing the city's pressing need for affordable childcare.

We created a program that trained women in the family shelter system to own, license, and operate small home daycare centers from their homes once they transitioned to permanent housing through Section 8. This wasn't just about creating jobs; it was about building futures. By partnering with the city and navigating the complex licensing process, we equipped these women with the tools to run sustainable businesses while providing quality childcare to families in their communities.

To amplify the program's impact, we worked with the city to allocate daycare vouchers, ensuring that the women's new businesses addressed the growing waitlist demand for affordable childcare in NYC. The program wasn't just transformative for the participants – it strengthened the city's childcare infrastructure, created economic opportunities, and provided a pathway out of poverty for families.

This initiative taught me the power of advocacy paired with action. By collaborating with local government, leveraging existing resources, and championing a bold vision, we turned a systemic challenge into a ripple effect of empowerment, opportunity, and community impact.

Here's your takeaway: advocacy isn't just about making noise; it's about making a difference. Whether it's reforming systems, creating programs, or amplifying voices, your efforts can create a legacy of impact that extends far beyond your business.

What's your cause? What's your platform? Step up, speak out, and lead the way. Because the change you inspire beyond your business can ripple out in ways you can't even imagine. And if Ben & Jerry's can do it with ice cream, imagine what you can do with your voice.

Inspiring Change in Your Community

Here's the truth: people are starving for leadership that doesn't just meet the bottom line but uplifts everyone it touches. Think about it – how often do we hear people talk wistfully about companies or leaders who genuinely care? What if you became that leader for your community? The one who listens, acts, and inspires others to think bigger and do better.

Start by looking around. What are the specific challenges your community faces? Maybe there's a lack of after-school programs, crumbling infrastructure, or small businesses struggling to stay afloat. Whatever the need, think about how your business can help fill the gap. This isn't about grand gestures or saving the world in one fell swoop – it's about showing up where it matters most.

Take Sweetgreen as an example. They started as a single salad shop in Washington, D.C., but quickly became a local staple, not just because of their food but because of their purpose. Sweetgreen didn't just sell salads; they hosted yoga classes in the park, partnered with local farmers, and created wellness events that brought people together. They showed their customers they cared about their health and their community. That kind of engagement turns customers into advocates and expands a business's impact far beyond its physical space.

Think about what you can do to create that kind of connection in your own community. Could you organize a mentorship program for local youth, helping them navigate career paths? Or perhaps you could rally your team for a neighborhood cleanup, demonstrating your commitment to making the streets you walk every day safer and more welcoming. Maybe your business has the resources to create jobs in underserved areas, becoming not just an employer but an anchor of opportunity.

Pause for a moment and imagine this: what if every leader reading this book – yes, that includes you – committed to championing net-positivity not just in their business but in their networks and communities? Think about the domino effect.

When businesses prioritize purpose, they set a new standard, forcing their competitors to step up. When leaders inspire, they awaken the potential in others. When communities see real, meaningful change, they begin to expect it everywhere. That's how transformation happens – not with one big wave but with countless ripples that grow stronger as they spread.

Here's the best part: you don't have to be perfect, and you definitely don't have to have it all figured out. The most powerful step you can take is the first one. Share your journey – the challenges, the missteps, the small victories. Build partnerships with those who share your values. Advocate for the changes you know your community needs.

Here's a story of how purpose and action can create profound change. I once worked with Catholic Big Sisters in New York City, where we launched a program aimed at transforming the future for first-generation immigrant girls. These young women often grew up with limited career role models, seeing their mothers working tirelessly as cashiers, nannies, or housekeepers because those were the only opportunities they knew. We wanted to challenge that narrative and expose them to a world of entrepreneurship and possibility.

The program focused on middle and high school girls, empowering them to create, launch, and operate small businesses. One standout project involved the girls developing a line of self-care products – bath salts, face masks, and lotions – that they sold as affordable and accessible pampering packages. The process wasn't just about selling products; it was about learning business planning, marketing, and teamwork. These young women gained skills that opened doors they didn't even know existed.

The knock-on effect was extraordinary. Not only did these girls see themselves as business owners and creators, but their families and communities began to see new possibilities too. They didn't have to follow a set path – they could create their own.

This example demonstrates how focusing on both purpose and action can create a lasting impact. When you invest in meaningful programs that align with your mission, you're not just solving immediate challenges – you're reshaping futures. That's the kind of leadership that inspires change far beyond your organization.

Before we move on, take a moment to ask yourself: *what kind of leader do I want to be remembered as? Am I building something that will last? Am I creating the kind of change that inspires others to follow in your footsteps?*

In Chapter 13, we'll tackle the final – and perhaps most meaningful – piece of the puzzle: your legacy. What does it mean to leave the world better than you found it? How do you ensure that the work you've done continues to make an impact long after you're gone?

Leadership isn't just about the next quarter or even the next decade. It's about building something extraordinary that stands the test of time.

Let's dive into the final stretch of this journey.

Together, we'll create not just a plan for today but a legacy for tomorrow.

Let's get to work. Your moment to lead the way is now.

> **KEY TAKEAWAYS**
>
> **Good leaders vs. great leaders**
>
> Be a great leader, one who inspires, connects, and empowers others to envision and achieve transformative change.
>
> - Share your story.
> - Be a connector.
> - Advocate beyond your business.
> - Inspire community change.
> - Create a ripple effect.
>
> Great leaders don't just lead their organizations – they inspire change across industries and communities. By sharing your story, building connections, and advocating for meaningful causes, you can create a legacy of impact and influence far beyond your business.

Creating a Legacy

Leaving a Lasting Impact on Your Business and the World

In 1858, a woman named Marianne Cope took a leap of faith that would change countless lives – but not in her lifetime. She was a German immigrant who became a nun and later ran some of the first hospitals in the United States that welcomed patients regardless of income, race, or disease. But her defining moment came when she answered a call to move to Hawaii to care for people with leprosy, a disease so feared that those diagnosed were exiled to live out their days in isolation.

Cope didn't hesitate. She and her sisters moved to the Kalaupapa colony on the island of Molokai, where they transformed a place of suffering into a thriving, dignified community. They built schools, homes, and hospitals. They didn't find a cure for leprosy – that wouldn't come for decades – but they planted the seeds of change that reshaped the way the world treated those with the disease.

She never sought recognition. She simply led with purpose. And over a century later, the world still remembers her name.

That's the power of legacy.

As the Greek proverb goes: "A society grows great when old men plant trees whose shade they know they shall never sit in."

It's not about being the loudest voice in the room. It's not about what you personally achieve – it's about the ripples you create that last far beyond your time.

Let me ask you: what will you leave behind? What will be your "shade tree" for future generations?

In this final chapter, we're not just talking about success – we're talking about significance. Your business, your leadership, and your decisions have the power to shape industries, communities, and lives for years to come.

Your legacy isn't just something you leave when you're gone – it's something you build every single day.

Let's make it count.

What Will You Be Remembered For?

Here's a question to start with: when all is said and done, what will people say about the work you've done? Not just in terms of profits or products, but the difference you've made in lives, communities, and even the world.

In 2022, I co-founded Hera Associates alongside a trusted colleague and lifelong friend, driven by a shared vision to create a consulting firm unlike any other. Hera Associates wasn't born out of convenience or circumstance – it was born out of a deep desire to tackle the complex social challenges of our time with boldness, creativity, and a commitment to lasting impact.

The name Hera wasn't chosen lightly. Hera, the Greek goddess of women, family, and community, symbolizes strength, unity, and the power of collective purpose. That spirit is at the core of everything we do. Hera Associates is a global social impact consulting firm designed to elevate purpose-driven leaders and organizations. We bridge private sector efficiency with nonprofit passion and international development expertise to create transformative solutions that not only address today's challenges but pave the way for a brighter future.

The "why" behind Hera Associates is deeply personal. After years of working in nonprofits, philanthropy, and international development, my co-founder and I recognized a glaring gap: too many organizations wanted to drive meaningful change but lacked the tools, partnerships, and strategies to make it sustainable. We wanted to be the bridge – to bring bold, actionable ideas to life while respecting and amplifying the unique strengths of the organizations we work with.

We built Hera Associates on values that matter to us: boldness, inclusion, integrity, and yes, even fun. One of our guiding principles is that the work of changing the world doesn't have to feel heavy all the time. Laughter, curiosity, and creativity fuel our solutions just as much as data and strategy do. We're serious about results, but we believe the journey should energize everyone involved.

Since launching, Hera Associates has worked with nonprofits, government agencies, and businesses around the world, co-creating strategies that generate social and financial impact. Whether it's helping a nonprofit scale its programs to serve more people or working with a midsize business to embed equity and sustainability into their operations, every project we take on reflects our mission: to build an inclusive and equitable world where everyone has the opportunity to thrive.

Let me tell you, founding Hera Associates wasn't without its challenges. There were late nights, tough decisions, and moments of doubt. But through it all, we stayed anchored to our mission. And now, as I look at the upshot of our work – stronger communities, more resilient organizations, and leaders stepping boldly into their roles – I'm reminded of why we started.

Hera Associates isn't just a consulting firm; it's a movement. It's a promise that business can and should be a force for good. As you think about your own legacy and the impact you want to leave, I hope our story serves as a reminder: when passion and purpose come together, the possibilities are endless.

Legacy isn't about plaques on walls or awards on shelves – it's about the enduring impact of your leadership.

Before we dive into strategy, let's take a moment to applaud where you are now. You've come a long way, from exploring your purpose to embedding it into your operations, measuring your impact, and empowering your team. You've built momentum.

Let's ensure it lasts.

Reflecting on Your Transformation: Celebrate the Wins

Pause for a moment. Reflect on your journey. Think about how far you've come since the start of this book. Maybe you've shifted how you think about leadership. Perhaps you've already implemented some changes, such as setting meaningful goals, creating a sustainability roadmap, or aligning your team around a shared purpose. Did it feel hard? Sure. Was it worth it? Absolutely.

When I first started at the YMCA of San Francisco, we were in crisis mode during the pandemic, but we turned empty facilities into emergency childcare centers for first responders. That wasn't just about short-term survival – it was about creating a blueprint for how an organization can pivot with purpose under pressure. It reminded me that celebrating progress, no matter how small, is a critical part of staying inspired.

So, here's your permission slip: celebrate what you've achieved so far. It's a big deal.

Envisioning Your Legacy: What's the Ripple Effect?

Every decision you make as a leader sends ripples through your business, your community, and beyond. Maybe you've empowered a team member who will go on to lead their own purpose-driven initiatives. Perhaps your sustainability efforts inspired another business in your industry to follow suit. The ripple effects of your leadership are likely more significant than you realize.

Take Unilever's Paul Polman, for example. His tenure as CEO transformed Unilever into a global leader in sustainability. When he left, the company didn't revert to old ways – it continued to build on the foundation he created. That's the hallmark of a strong legacy: when your impact outlasts your presence.

Ask yourself: *what ripples do I want to create? What systems, values, and initiatives can I put in place now that will endure?*

Strategies for Ensuring Long-Term Impact

Building a legacy isn't just about the big, splashy moves – it's about embedding your purpose into the DNA of your organization.

Here's how:

1. **Build systems, not dependencies:** You don't want your impact to disappear the moment you step away. Focus on creating systems, not just initiatives. For example, during my time working with the City of New York, we developed programs that trained women in shelters to become licensed childcare providers. The beauty of that program? It was sustainable. It didn't rely on one person or one team – it had the infrastructure to keep running and evolving.

2. **Develop your successors:** Your greatest legacy might not be the work you do – it could be the leaders you inspire. Invest in mentoring and developing the next generation of purpose-driven leaders. Imagine what they could achieve if they had your guidance now.

One of the most rewarding aspects of leadership – and something I never take for granted – is hearing from former team members who reach out to say thank you. It's a feeling unlike any other. Out of the blue, I'll get a call, email, or text from someone I worked with years ago, telling me that my leadership made a difference in their career or even their life.

In fact, just this morning, I received a text from a staff member I worked with seven years ago. Her message read: *You were the best supervisor I've ever had.* I can't tell you how much that meant to me – not because I need the validation, but because it reinforces that the way we show up as leaders matters. It's proof that taking the time to mentor, guide, and empower people leaves a lasting impact that goes far beyond the job.

Even on the harder days – because let's face it, leadership isn't always smooth sailing – those moments remind me why I do what I do. I'll never forget my final days as Executive Director at one company when I was saying goodbye to an incredible team. A member of the leadership team pulled me aside and said something that will stick with me forever – "I've learned more from you during your tenure than I have in my entire career from anyone else." That blew me away. It wasn't about a single moment or project – it was about everything that had led up to it: the mentorship, the trust, the investment in her growth.

Hearing those words reminded me that leadership isn't just about the milestones we hit; it's about the people we empower along the way. Moments like that show how even the most challenging seasons can leave behind a legacy of growth and connection.

That's the kind of legacy that gets me pumped up. It's not about the titles I've held or the goals I've achieved; it's about the people I've had the privilege to work alongside. Knowing that my leadership helped someone grow in their career, believe in themselves, or approach challenges differently is what keeps me inspired. And it's a powerful reminder that as leaders, the seeds we plant today often bloom years later, sometimes when we least expect it.

Leadership isn't just about meeting quarterly targets or managing budgets. It's about leaving people better than you found them. When I reflect on my legacy, I don't think about the strategies or projects (although those matter, too) – I think about the people. Because at the end of the day, your legacy as a leader is written in the stories of the people you've empowered, the growth you've inspired, and the ripple effects of your time together. And that, to me, is the ultimate reward.

Bake Purpose into Your Culture

Purpose is the real heartbeat of your business. It should influence everything, from how decisions are made to how your team connects with the mission on a daily basis. A truly purpose-driven culture goes beyond posters in the break room or occasional volunteer events. It's about embedding your values into the DNA of your company, so they guide every action, interaction, and decision.

Here's how:

- **Create purposeful traditions and rituals:** rituals and traditions are powerful tools for reinforcing your mission. They create shared experiences that remind your team why they show up every day – and why it matters.

    For instance:
    - *Patagonia's activist sabbaticals:* by giving employees time to volunteer with environmental causes, Patagonia reinforces its mission of stewardship while empowering its team to live those values personally.

- *Warby Parker's impact meetings:* this eyewear company holds regular meetings to share stories of how their "buy a pair, give a pair" model has changed lives, keeping their team connected to the global impact of their work.
- *Zappos' core value celebrations:* Zappos takes its quirky, customer-focused culture seriously, hosting events and awards to recognize employees who embody the company's core values.

Action tip: start small! Establish a monthly "mission moment" at staff meetings, where team members share how their work aligns with your purpose. Or create an annual day of service where the entire team contributes to a cause tied to your mission.

- **Embed purpose in professional development:** your team will be more motivated to embrace your mission if they see it reflected in their own growth. Align professional development with purpose by:
  - *Offering purpose-driven training:* for example, Starbucks provides sustainability training for baristas, teaching them about the company's coffee sourcing practices and environmental goals.
  - *Encouraging personal projects:* Google's "20% Time" policy, which allows employees to dedicate part of their time to passion projects, fosters innovation and keeps purpose alive across the organization.
  - *Connecting individual goals to the mission:* when you show employees how their personal ambitions align with organizational purpose, you cultivate deeper engagement. For example, a team member in marketing might spearhead a campaign highlighting your social impact.

  Action tip: during one-on-ones, ask your employees how their roles can better align with their personal values or the organization's purpose. Use their feedback to identify opportunities for growth.

- **Reward and recognize purpose-driven actions:** people love to feel appreciated, and they thrive when they see their work contributing

to something bigger. Create recognition programs that highlight purpose-driven actions, such as:
- Employee awards for living out company values.
- Sharing impact stories in newsletters or team meetings.
- Providing perks, such as additional PTO or donation matches, for employees who volunteer or go above and beyond to support your mission.
- Ben & Jerry's takes recognition a step further by celebrating suppliers that embody the company's values. For instance, they highlight Fair Trade suppliers and community-driven initiatives in their annual impact report, showcasing how partners align with their mission.

Action tip: consider creating an annual "Purpose Champion" award in your organization to recognize employees who have made outstanding contributions to advancing your mission.

- **Build purpose into onboarding:** first impressions matter. Onboarding is a critical moment to immerse new employees in your culture and purpose, for example:
  - TOMS Shoes includes a session in their onboarding program where new hires learn about the impact of their "One for One" model.
  - Junior Achievement integrates its mission into onboarding by having every new employee serve as a volunteer lead for at least one program. As a volunteer-led financial literacy and entrepreneurship powerhouse, Junior Achievement ensures its staff experience the mission firsthand by teaching in classrooms, empowering young minds to understand money, business, and the power of their potential. This approach not only reinforces the organization's core values but also fosters immediate connection and pride among new team members.

Action tip: consider incorporating hands-on mission experiences into your onboarding process. Whether it's volunteering, shadowing frontline staff, or attending community events, immersing employees in your purpose from day one builds alignment and enthusiasm that sticks. Or if that feels like too much, consider creating a "Purpose Playbook" for new hires that outlines your mission, values, and impact stories, giving them a clear sense of how their role contributes to the bigger picture.

Document the Journey

Write down what worked, what didn't, and what you learned along the way. This isn't just about preserving your legacy; it's about giving future leaders a roadmap to build on. Share your insights in a way that others can learn and grow from them.

Here's how some businesses have nailed this:

- Pixar, known for its creative storytelling, has a unique process they call the "Braintrust." After every film project, the team documents what worked in their creative process and what didn't. These insights are shared across teams and become part of Pixar's institutional knowledge, ensuring every movie benefits from the lessons of the last one. This practice has contributed to their string of animated hits, from Toy Story to Soul.
- Nike doesn't just focus on producing innovative athletic gear – they also document their journey toward sustainability. Through their annual Impact Report, Nike transparently shares successes, setbacks, and next steps toward their goals, such as reducing carbon emissions and eliminating waste. By publishing these insights, Nike not only holds itself accountable but also inspires other brands to follow suit.
- Patagonia's Worn Wear program, which promotes repair and reuse over buying new, grew out of years of trial and error. The company documents the lessons learned from pilot projects, customer feedback, and operational challenges, using these insights to refine and scale the program. They share these stories with their audience,

furthering their environmental mission while inspiring a culture of thoughtful consumption.

How You Can Document Your Journey

- **Keep a leadership journal:** make it a habit to record key decisions, challenges, and outcomes. What did you learn? How did your team grow? Reflecting in real-time provides clarity and creates a resource for future leaders.
- **Create case studies:** turn milestones and projects into case studies. Highlight the strategies you used, the impact you achieved, and the lessons learned. Share these with your team or broader industry to inspire others.
- **Write an annual legacy report:** treat it like an impact report, but for your leadership. What goals did you set? What progress did you make? What areas need improvement? This not only provides a roadmap for future leaders but also keeps you accountable to your mission.

Documenting doesn't have to be daunting. Start by jotting down lessons after major projects or initiatives. As you build the habit, consider creating a "Leadership Legacy Handbook" or even a blog or vlog to share your insights more broadly.

Remember, your story doesn't just belong to you – it's a guide for those who will continue the journey you started.

Stay Curious and Flexible

Your legacy isn't a static finish line – it's a living, breathing entity that adapts as the world around shifts. Staying curious and flexible is the hallmark of great leaders who understand that success isn't just about solving today's problems but also preparing for what's next. Let's explore how some of the most forward-thinking business leaders have embodied this philosophy and built legacies that continue to thrive.

Jeff Bezos famously built Amazon on the principle of being "stubborn on vision but flexible on details." What started as an online bookstore quickly grew into an e-commerce giant because Bezos remained curious about what customers wanted. Amazon Prime, AWS (Amazon Web Services), and even the development of cashier-less stores such as Amazon Go showcase a willingness to pivot and adapt to emerging opportunities. Bezos's approach teaches us that curiosity about unmet needs and flexibility to pursue them can lead to transformative growth.

Oprah Winfrey didn't stop at dominating daytime television. When she recognized the decline of traditional media, she pivoted, launching her OWN (Oprah Winfrey Network) and expanding her reach into digital platforms and streaming content. Oprah's ability to adapt to changing audience behaviors while staying true to her purpose – empowering and inspiring people – ensured her relevance across generations.

When Satya Nadella became CEO of Microsoft, the company was stuck in a competitive rut. Nadella's leadership ushered in a culture of curiosity and learning, shifting the focus from internal rivalry to collaboration. By embracing cloud computing, open-source technology, and partnerships (even with competitors), Nadella positioned Microsoft as a leader in innovation. His mantra? "Hit refresh." It's a reminder that even well-established organizations need to stay flexible to stay ahead.

So how might you foster curiosity and flexibility in your leadership?

1. **Ask the right questions**

    Adopt a mindset of continuous learning by regularly asking – what's next?

    Or, what if? Encourage your team to do the same.

    - *Example:* Reed Hastings, the co-founder of Netflix, constantly asks, "What will our customers want in five or ten years?" That forward-thinking approach helped Netflix evolve from DVD rentals to streaming and eventually to producing award-winning original content.

2. **Be willing to pivot**
   Flexibility doesn't mean abandoning your mission; it means exploring new paths to achieve it.
   - *Example:* Howard Schultz of Starbucks led the company through a major pivot when he returned as CEO in 2008. By refocusing on the customer experience – closing stores for barista training and redesigning coffee shops – he revitalized the brand and brought Starbucks back to its roots.

3. **Encourage experimentation**
   Foster a culture where your team feels safe to innovate and test new ideas, even if they fail.
   - *Example:* Google's "20% Time" initiative allows employees to spend 20 percent of their workweek on passion projects. This practice has led to groundbreaking innovations like Gmail and Google Maps
   - *Action tip:* schedule a "Curiosity Day." Dedicate one day a month to exploring new ideas, technologies, or market trends, with your team. Use it as an opportunity to brainstorm how your business can evolve.

     For example:
     - What's a new technology that could enhance your operations?
     - How are customer preferences changing, and what can you do to stay ahead?
     - What's a bold initiative you could try in the next quarter?

Curiosity isn't just a trait – it's a discipline. And flexibility isn't a sign of weakness – it's a strength. As you lead with these principles, you'll build a legacy that's not only impactful but also dynamic, ensuring your work continues to thrive and inspire long after you've passed the torch.

A Personal Reflection: Leadership as a Journey

One of the most impactful moments in my leadership journey came through Hera Associates' work on a government contract aimed at integrating DEIAJ (Diversity, Equity, Inclusion, Accessibility, and Justice) principles into the climate sector. The task was monumental – ensuring that a traditionally exclusive field became more representative, inclusive, and equitable while tackling one of the most pressing issues of our time.

We started by listening. Through stakeholder engagement sessions, we heard from underrepresented voices within the environmental workforce – women, people of color, and those from economically disadvantaged communities – who had been historically excluded from decision-making processes. Their insights weren't just eye-opening; they were transformative. Together, we co-created a framework that not only addressed representation in the climate workforce but also embedded DEIAJ principles into policies, hiring practices, and community engagement strategies.

Months later, I received an email from a young environmental scientist who shared how this project had opened doors for her career. She told me that because of the programs we helped establish, she was now leading a local initiative to engage marginalized communities in renewable energy projects. That's when it hit me: leadership isn't about the immediate results you see – it's about creating systems and opportunities that enable others to thrive long after you've stepped away.

And here's what I've learned: leadership, especially in complex sectors such as climate and DEIAJ, is an evolving practice. It's not about solving one problem and moving on; it's about building frameworks that adapt as the world changes. At Hera Associates, we constantly remind our clients – and ourselves – that creating lasting impact means staying curious, staying engaged, and always asking: what's next?

This experience reinforced for me that leadership is about more than delivering results on a single contract. It's about creating ripples of change that expand beyond the immediate project, influencing industries, empowering individuals, and shifting mindsets. It's the kind of work that keeps me inspired and deeply motivated every single day.

Creating a Legacy: Leaving a Lasting Impact on Your Business and the World

This is it – the grand finale. But let's be clear: while this is the final section of the final chapter of this book, it's only the beginning of your journey. Over the past chapters, we've delved into what it takes to lead with purpose, foster collaboration, measure what matters, and embed net-positivity into the very essence of your business. You've equipped yourself with tools, strategies, and inspiration to align profit with purpose, to drive meaningful change, and to inspire others to do the same.

It's time to ask yourself the ultimate questions:

What legacy will I leave?

Will my business be remembered as one that thrived while making a difference?

Will my leadership inspire others to reimagine what success looks like?

Will the ripple effects of my efforts redefine industries, uplift communities, and make our world more equitable and sustainable?

Reflecting on the Journey

Take a moment to celebrate how far you've come. You've confronted big ideas, tackled hard truths, and embraced the opportunity to rethink what "business as usual" could be. Along the way, you've championed strategies that prioritize collaboration, equity, and sustainability. Whether through transforming your operations, inspiring your team, or engaging your community, you've shown that business can – and should – be a force for good.

But here's the thing: a legacy isn't a moment in time. It's not just one bold decision or a single success story. A legacy is built over time, through the choices you make every day, the people you empower, and the systems you create to ensure that your vision endures.

This journey has always been about something bigger – about reshaping "business as usual" into something truly extraordinary: net-positivity.

A Call to Action: Your Role as a Leader

This is your moment to lead. You've gathered the tools, the insights, and the strategies to make a lasting impact. It's time to put them into action. Start where you are – with the resources you have today – and take the next step toward embedding purpose into every layer of your business.

Remember, this isn't a journey you have to take alone.

At Hera Associates, we've built our work around helping leaders like you transform their businesses, industries, and communities. Whether it's helping businesses and corporations integrate purpose into their core strategies, guiding nonprofits to measure their impact, or partnering with governments to address complex challenges, we are here to amplify your efforts and support your success.

Looking for more?

- Visit our website to explore our resources: www.hera-associates.com
- Connect with a consultant: www.hera-associates.com/contact
- Or join a network of leaders who, like you, are championing net-positivity: www.linkedin.com/company/hera-associates-llc

Together, we can redefine what it means to succeed in business, proving that purpose and profit are not only compatible but inseparable.

The Final Word: Your Legacy Starts Now

As you close this book, take a moment to reflect on the leader you're becoming. Leadership isn't about perfection – it's about progress. It's about standing firm in your values, showing up when it's hard, and making choices that reflect the world you want to create.

Imagine a world where businesses prioritize net-positivity – where success is measured not just by profits but by the lives touched, communities strengthened, and ecosystems restored. That's the future we're building, one decision at a time.

So, here's your challenge:

- Lead boldly.
- Collaborate fearlessly.
- Keep learning, growing, and inspiring.

Your legacy begins now!

The world is ready for leaders like you – leaders who understand that doing good is good business. Together, we can make a lasting impact, proving that businesses built on purpose are not just sustainable – they're unstoppable.

Take a deep breath, savor this moment, and let's get to work.

The journey doesn't end here – it's just beginning.

KEY TAKEAWAYS

Define your legacy

Build a legacy of purpose, collaboration, and positive impact that continues to thrive and inspire long after you've moved on.

Your journey starts now.

- Celebrate progress.
- Create systems for sustainability.
- Embed purpose in culture.
- Document and share your journey.
- Foster curiosity and flexibility.
- Create a ripple effect.

Call to action

Lead boldly and align profit with purpose. Your legacy begins with intentional, everyday actions that reflect your values.

Conclusion
Leading the Future

Your Impact Starts Now

The future is yours to shape.

When we began this journey together, I posed a simple yet profound question: what if businesses could align profit with purpose – and thrive because of it?

As we reach the final pages of this book, I hope you see that the answer is not only yes, but that it's already happening – in businesses of every size, across industries, and led by people just like you.

We've explored real-world examples of companies that have woven impact into their operations – businesses that don't just talk about sustainability, equity, and social good, but embed it into their DNA. We've broken down the myths that say purpose and profit can't coexist. And most importantly, we've equipped you with a framework that proves impact isn't just an add-on or a marketing gimmick – it's a strategic advantage.

From Intention to Action

If there's one thing that I hope you take away from this book, it's that leading with purpose isn't just for industry giants or billion-dollar brands. Whether you're running a startup, a nonprofit, or a corporation, you already have the tools to create a net-positive business.

Success in today's world isn't about chasing short-term wins. It's about building something that lasts. It's about showing up every day and making intentional choices – about how you lead, how you invest, how you innovate, and how you leave things better than you found them.

It doesn't matter whether you're implementing sustainability initiatives, strengthening community partnerships, or rethinking how your company measures success. What matters is that you start. Because the real impact of your leadership won't be measured in quarterly earnings alone – it will be measured in the lives you touch, the cultures you shape, and the legacy you leave behind.

Your Legacy Begins Now

Remember the stories we explored – leaders who redefined what was possible, organizations that pivoted in moments of crisis, businesses that chose to lead instead of follow. Their success wasn't built on luck. It was built on courage, clarity, and commitment.

Now, it's your turn.

As you step away from these pages and back into your role – whether that's as a founder, an executive, a strategist, or a changemaker – you carry with you the power to lead differently. The power to build something that outlasts you.

Because in the end, the most successful businesses aren't just the ones that generate the most profit – they're the ones that leave the greatest impact.

The question is no longer if you can do this.

The question is: **how bold will you be?**

The future of business belongs to those who are willing to redefine it.

So go forward, lead with purpose, and build the legacy only you can create.

The world is waiting.

Let's get to work!

Your Next Step: Book a Free Clarity Call

As a thank you for reading, we're offering you a **FREE 30-minute clarity call** – a one-on-one session to assess your current strategy and uncover clear next steps. Schedule through the QR code or link below.

www.calendly.com/jrider-hera-associates/30min

In your Clarity Call, we'll help you:

- Evaluate your current position using the **Net-Positivity Framework**
- Spot opportunities to better align profit with purpose
- Receive expert insights tailored to your organization
- Get answers to your biggest questions around strategy, sustainability, and growth

Let's Keep the Momentum Going

If this book sparked new ideas or challenged the way you think about purpose and profit, I'd be honored if you'd leave a review. Your words help more readers discover this work – and take action in their own businesses and communities.

Ready to go deeper?

- **Book a keynote, panelist, or tailored work session** to inspire and equip your team or audience: www.hera-associates.com/contact
- **Schedule a consultation call** to explore how Hera Associates can help your organization grow with strategy and lead with purpose: calendly.com/jrider-hera-associates/30min
- **Buy or gift this book** to a forward-thinking leader ready to make a net-positive impact: www.amazon.com/author/jenniferrider

Let's build a more sustainable, equitable, and profitable future – together.

www.hera-associates.com/book-review

Acknowledgments

Writing a book is never a solo endeavor. It takes a community – a network of supporters, challengers, and believers who push you forward even when doubt creeps in. This book would not exist without the people who encouraged me, challenged me, and reminded me why this work matters.

To my launch team – for championing this book, spreading the word, and making sure it reaches the people who need it most. Your support means the world to me.

To my mom – who always believed in my natural leadership and never let me forget it. You saw my strengths before I did and pushed me to recognize and embrace them.

To Stefanie – who always makes sure I know that I am smart, competent, and have important things to say. Your confidence in me is a gift I treasure.

To Kyan – my greatest motivator, my daily inspiration. You make me want to do better, be better, and leave the world better.

To Claudia – who constantly reminds me to recognize opportunity, go after what I want, and never settle.

To my colleagues – who saw the power in my "different" way of thinking and encouraged me to step into that power. You know who you are, and your validation gave me the courage to own my voice.

This book is a reflection of all the lessons, encouragement, and challenges that have shaped me. To everyone who played a role in this journey – thank you. Your impact on my life and work is immeasurable.

About the Author

Jennifer Rider, MBA, MSEd, is a nationally recognized executive, strategist, and social impact leader transforming the way businesses balance profit and purpose. A recipient of the 2024 & 2025 Great Companies International Women Entrepreneur Award, she is known for crafting sustainable business strategies that drive large-scale impact.

With an MBA from Rollins College Crummer Graduate School of Business and a master's in education and counseling psychology from the University of Southern California, Jennifer bridges business strategy, social impact, and operational excellence. She has led multi-million-dollar organizations and held executive roles including CEO of Big Brothers Big Sisters of Central Florida, Senior Executive Director at the YMCA of San Francisco, Vice President of Development for Junior Achievement of Northern California, and Regional Director at the Anti-Defamation League.

As co-founder of Hera Associates, a global consulting firm specializing in purpose-driven strategy, Jennifer helps businesses, nonprofits, and government agencies embed sustainability, equity, and social responsibility into their operations. Her work spans state and federal contracts, corporate social impact initiatives, and strategic advisory for high-growth organizations.

Jennifer is also a sought-after speaker, available for keynotes, panels, and workshops on building net-positive businesses and purpose-driven leadership.

Connect Jennifer

@ jrider@hera-associates.com

🌐 www.hera-associates.com

in www.linkedin.com/in/riderjennifer/

www.ingramcontent.com/pod-product-compliance
Lightning Source LLC
Chambersburg PA
CBHW020524080526
44583CB00013B/730